MARCO  POLO

Insider Tips

ALGARVE

ATLANTIC
OCEAN

Bordeaux

PORTUGAL

AND

Lisbon

Madrid

Algarve

SPAIN

Balearic
Islands

Faro

Tangier

Mediterranean
Sea

MOROCCO

6 **INSIDER TIPS**
Our top 15 Insider Tips

8 **BEST OF...**
● Great places for free
● Only in the Algarve
● And if it rains?
● Relax and chill out

12 **INTRODUCTION**
Discover the Algarve!

18 **WHAT'S HOT**
There are lots of new things to
discover in the Algarve

20 **IN A NUTSHELL**
Background information on the
Algarve

26 **FOOD & DRINK**
Top culinary tips

30 **SHOPPING**
For a fun-filled shopping spree!

32 **THE BARLAVENTO**
32 Albufeira
39 Lagos
44 Portimão
51 Sagres

56 **THE SOTAVENTO**
56 Faro
63 Tavira
67 Vilamoura
71 Vila Real de Santo António

74 **THE HINTERLAND**
74 Loulé
78 Monchique & the Serra
82 Silves

SYMBOLS

INSIDERTIP Insider Tip

★ Highlight

●●●● Best of...

☼ Scenic view

♲ Responsible travel: fair-
trade principles and the
environment respected

**PRICE CATEGORIES
HOTELS**

Expensive over 140 euros

Moderate 90–140 euros

Budget under 90 euros

Price for a double room with
breakfast in the high season

**PRICE CATEGORIES
RESTAURANTS**

Expensive over 22 euros

Moderate 15–22 euros

Budget under 15 euros

Price for a menu without
drinks

On the cover: The heritage of the Moors lives on: Loulé p. 74 | A fish feast fit for a king p. 45

CONTENTS

86 THE WEST COAST
86 Aljezur
89 Cabo de São Vicente

92 DISCOVERY TOURS
92 Algarve at a glance
99 At one with nature: the wild west
102 Castles and more: the undiscovered east
105 Through the unspoilt hinterland

112 TRAVEL WITH KIDS
Best things to do with kids

116 FESTIVALS & EVENTS
All dates at a glance

118 LINKS, BLOGS, APPS & MORE
Plan ahead and use on the go

120 TRAVEL TIPS
From A to Z

126 USEFUL PHRASES

130 ROAD ATLAS

108 SPORTS & ACTIVITIES
Activities for all seasons

146 INDEX & CREDITS

148 DOS & DON'TS

DID YOU KNOW?
Timeline → p. 14
Local specialities → p. 28
Algarve wine → p. 47
The Algarve on a bike → p. 52
Ria Formosa → p. 64
Books & films → p. 68
Medronho → p. 78
National holidays → p. 117
Budgeting → p. 123
Currency converter → p. 124
Weather in Faro → p. 125

MAPS IN THE GUIDEBOOK
(124 A1) Page numbers and coordinates refer to the road atlas
(0) Site/address located off the map
Coordinates are also given for places that are not marked on the road atlas.

(*Ω A1*) refers to the removable pull-out map

INSIDE FRONT COVER:
The best Highlights

INSIDE BACK COVER:
City maps of Albufeira, Faro, Lagos and Tavira

The best
MARCO POLO
Insider Tips

Our top 15 Insider Tips

INSIDER TIP **Nature reserve trip**
The 60 km/37 miles long *Ria Formosa* lagoon is a tidal water world and an important nature reserve. A sailing boat or kayak ride is an excellent way to discover its beauty → **p. 60**

INSIDER TIP **More than just salt**
The exceptional quality of the *flor do sal* or salt flower from the Algarve has made it the world's finest salt delicacy – stock up on it while you're here! → **p. 31**

INSIDER TIP **Gateway to the city**
The remains of Lagos' city wall can be appreciated best at its most picturesque gateway *Arco de São Gonçalo* → **p. 40**

INSIDER TIP **Ria harbour zone**
Follow the signposts to the *Zona Ribeirinha* from the harbour in Alvor to enjoy beautiful views of the Ria de Alvor, the harboured yachts as well as bars and restaurants → **p. 49**

INSIDER TIP **Dolphin watching**
If you take one of the *dolphin watching* trips such as those on offer at the marina in Lagos, you have an excellent chance of spotting dolphins – and when they leap out of the water, have your camera ready to catch the look of amazement on the children's faces (photo right) → **p. 110**

INSIDER TIP **Medieval festival**
The era of the Saracens and the Crusades is rekindled at the Silves fortress in August. Every day a different scene is enacted and visitors amble through the market clad in attire from the Middle Ages → **p. 117**

INSIDER TIP **Stay in an old mill**
A Mediterranean atmosphere is what characterises the restored 16th century mill complex of *Moinho do Pedro*. With the hill in Algoz as your vantage point, get a view all the way from Lagos to Albufeira Monchique → **p. 85**

INSIDER TIP Culinary surprises

Ana Miguel rules over the pots and pans in the *Perdição* restaurant's kitchen in Loulé – however to enjoy her surprise menu, you have to reserve a table in advance → **p. 77**

INSIDER TIP Clifftop walk

Follow the path over the *Praia do Carvoeiro* to Algar Seco to breathe in the sea air and enjoy splendid views over this captivating landscape → **p. 50**

INSIDER TIP Family refuge

Casa da Mãe in Salir has delightful holiday apartments, a pool and plenty of rest to offer its guests → **p. 78**

INSIDER TIP Lookout point

The ruins of the *Fortaleza de Santa Catarina* are just one of the Algarve's many coastal lookout points, a tiny fort in Praia da Rocha offering beautiful views → **p. 51**

INSIDER TIP Rural revival

Once a deserted rural village, *Pedralva* is now experiencing a Renaissance of sorts thanks to the work of a local action group – stay in one of the beautifully renovated village houses → **p. 91**

INSIDER TIP A breath of fresh air...

...offers a stroll along the sea front *promenade* lined with palm trees and hanging lanterns at the beach and tourist resort of Luz (photo left) → **p. 44**

INSIDER TIP Artistic pleasure

The *Galeria Arte Algarve* offers two impressive spectacles for visitors: its impressive location in an old wine storehouse and its ambitiously bold exhibitions, especially in summer → **p. 51**

INSIDER TIP Coastal gem

Lagoon beach, tiny harbour, picturesque sights – *Fuseta* combines all of this and more → **p. 66**

BEST OF...

GREAT PLACES FOR FREE
Discover new places and save money

FOR FREE

● *Expedition to the lagoon*
The lagoon of Ria Formosa is one of the largest natural treasures in the Algarve. The nature reserve's information centre at Olhão offers an *educational trail* where you can admire the beauty of the lagoon's landscape and which takes you past a tidal mill, Roman salt works and ruins → p. 114

● *Direct sourcing of fruit*
Do your bit to support the local population currently suffering from the economic crisis: Some locals now sell produce they have picked from their fruit trees or vegetable patches at rock-bottom prices directly in front of their houses → p. 39

● *Collect cockles and clams*
At low tide connoisseurs comb through the sands of the Ria de Alvor and on Armona Island for *ameijoas* (clams) and *berbigões* (cockles). To prepare: wash, heat well in a pot, add garlic and white wine – and voila, dinner is served! (photo) → p. 63

● *Chapel with artistic tiles*
Not every church in the Algarve offers free admission but the *Ermida Nossa Senhora da Conceição* in the historic centre of Loulé does: Adorned with the most spectacular azulejos, you can enjoy this delightful chapel for free → p. 82

● *Hilltop castle*
The *Castelo* perched on top of the hill in Tavira is a real eyecatcher from which you can take in the views all around. The fortress offers free access to visitors through the castle's gardens → p. 64

● *Water straight from the source*
The Serra de Monchique is the source of natural *spring waters.* Do what the locals do and fill your bottles and canisters at the taps where the water is drawn → p. 82

ONLY IN THE ALGARVE
Unique experiences

● **The culinary art of the Cataplana**
Cataplana is both a dish and the name of the copper pan it is prepared in. A sort of domed wok, it is perfect for preparing the delicious fresh seafood typical of the region, as in many restaurants in Sagres (photo) → **p. 27**

● **Beaches, beaches**
Here you will find more Blue Flags – the award that guarantees cleanliness and safety – than anywhere else in Europe. The superb beaches have fine golden white sand and easy access into the water. The showcase beach has to be the *Praia da Rocha* in Portimão → **p. 46**

● **Postcard perfect**
Fishing boats and bright colours: Even the big cutters that one comes across in every harbour are a display of colour. Unparalleled for its picture-perfect look has to be *Sagres harbour* → **p. 52**

● **Small works of art**
The *azulejos,* painted ceramic tiles, are said to be Portugal's most beautiful art. Their name and origin dates back to the Moors. *Az-zulayi* means "small stone". They decorate courtyards and hospitals, churches and chapels like the *Igreja de São Lourenço* in Almancil → **p. 69**

● **Firewater from the mountains**
Strawberries on bushes? The floury fruit of the strawberry tree looks convincingly like a strawberry. Yet they are not eaten, but cultivated for *medronho*. Try it (for example in the mountains around Monchique): Once distilled, the strong spirit has a superb taste → **p. 78**

● **Golfers' paradise**
The word Algarve is synonymous with the word golf. The sunny region has developed into a golfers' paradise with almost 40 golf courses to its name. Be it under pine trees or with a sea view – you can hole everywhere → **p. 110**

● **Surfers' haven**
Because huge waves generate huge fun, surfers are drawn to the Atlantic coast all year round – conditions there are also sought after by windsurfers and kite surfers. Top hot spot: *Praia da Bordeira* → **p. 111**

ONLY IN

BEST OF...

AND IF IT RAINS?
Activities to brighten your day

● **Beach pubs**
Wooden snack bars can be found on just about every beach. Here you can sit for hours, have a few drinks, read, or simply take time out to daydream. If the weather changes and the sea is rough, *Praia da Galé's* beach restaurants present a particularly cosy place to seek shelter → p. 35

● **Shopping**
They turn into people magnets on rainy days: the shopping centres *Algarve Shopping* in Guia, *Forum Algarve* in Faro (photo) and the *Aqua Portimão.* Shops, restaurants, supermarkets, cinemas and more → p. 37, 59

● **An unvarnished portrait of a hard life**
Inside beautiful industrial architecture in a restored fish factory, the *Museu de Portimão* depicts the traditional fishing life with many photos, fishing utensils and good museum didactics → p. 45

● **Our universe**
Faro is host to the *Centro Ciência Viva do Algarve.* Focal to this modern science centre is the observation of the universe and the oceans. Plenty of hi-tech equipment and interactive materials also describe environmental damage. There's no better way to understand nature → p. 57

● **More than just a local museum**
There are lots of things to see and do in the *Museu do Traje* in São Brás de Alportel: the museum's display of traditional dress and costumes, a cork exhibition in an adjacent building and last but not least the museum's bar → p. 62

● **Shelter in the convent**
The splendid cloister and the rest of the complex offer excellent shelter from the rain: Once a convent, the *Convento Nossa Senhora da Assunção* in the old part of Faro now houses the city's museum → p. 58

RAIN

RELAX AND CHILL OUT
Take it easy and spoil yourself

● *Pure and relaxing enjoyment*
Visit the island of Culatra (photo) to experience a world away from the typical Algarve and finish your stay with a culinary treat: Enjoy the freshest fish on the terrace of the *Januca* fish restaurant while soaking up the view over the water → **p. 60**

● *Sauna und pool*
Guests love the indoor relaxation oasis at Albufeira's *Epic Sana* hotel overlooking the Praia da Falésia. The large indoor pool is open 24x7 while a sauna and steam bath is available in the smaller pool → **p. 36**

● *Food for the soul*
Yoga at *Quinta da Calma* in Almancil relaxes the body and the mind – as does the heavenly calmness in this small village with its many more offers of relaxing therapies → **p. 69**

● *Refuge in nature*
Smells from the pine trees around, a palm garden and a circular swimming pool in which the skies over the Mata Nacional nature reserve are reflected: The *Casa dos Sonhos* is a true hideaway in the best sense of the word → **p. 43**

● *An all-time high*
Pack a picnic and take a drive to Arrifana and take advantage of the lookouts at the Castelo ruin. Especially at sunset you get a magnificent view of the majestic cliffs in the north and the crescent shaped bay of Arrifana in the south → **p. 89**

● *Sunset special*
The *O Castelo* at Faro protected by its city walls has the perfect geographical setting. Come here to soak up the scenic atmosphere while the sun sets slowly in the background → **p. 59**

INTRODUCTION

DISCOVER
THE ALGARVE!

Clean seawater, fresh air for deep breaths, heavenly beaches, natural bays, sheltered coves, rocky cliffs, barrier islands and a subtropical climate: This place ticks all the criteria for those hungry for a holiday – and it is only a two-and-a-half to three hour flight from the UK. It is no wonder that this coastal region on the south-western outskirts of Europe is a premier holiday destination for tourists from around the world!

The Algarve stretches across a 150 km/93 miles span from Spain to the Atlantic west coast. Nature has split the 50 km/31 miles deep coastal strip in two. To the west is the *Barlavento* characterised by a dramatic rocky coast and to the east, the *Sotavento*, defined by endless sandy beaches, dunes and lagoons. This is what attracts both sporting enthusiasts and families with children to one of the most beautiful regions of Europe who come not only for the Algarve's climate and coastline. The Algarve *hinterland* is made for fitness and nature lovers, for undertaking hikes and cycling tours. All this while up until a few decades ago the delights of the Algarve were unexplored even by the Portuguese people themselves and it was thought to be "at the edge of the world" somewhere in the direction of Africa. The only activ-

The Algarve in the evening: a stroll and a good meal in the old town of Lagos

ity was in the harbour towns, and those residents not involved in the fishing industry were engaged in agriculture. Hard to believe now that the donkey or mule was the main means of transport for many villagers until well into the 1970s!

The local inhabitants, the Algarvios, come across as Mediterranean, however they are a cultural mix with influences from North Africa and the Arab world, a legacy from when the Iberian peninsula was conquered by the Moors in the 8th century. They called the coastal strip of their new kingdom with its abundant sunshine "al Garb" (the west – as seen from Córdoba, the seat of the caliphate) from which the word Algarve originated. With their knowledge of agriculture and science they brought about a *truly advanced civilisation* characterised by active trade and religious tolerance. In the course of half a century they became integrated with the local population.

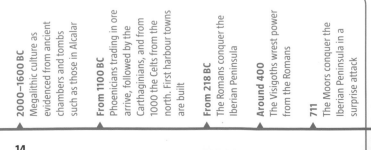

2000–1600 BC
Megalithic culture as evidenced from ancient chambers and tombs such as those in Alcalar

From 1100 BC
Phoenicians trading in ore arrive, followed by the Carthaginians, and from 1000 the Celts from the north. First harbour towns are built

From 218 BC
The Romans conquer the Iberian Peninsula

Around 400
The Visigoths wrest power from the Romans

711
The Moors conquer the Iberian Peninsula in a surprise attack

Sadly very few buildings from the Moorish era remain intact because so much was destroyed by the Christians when they conquered the area again in the *Reconquista*. The Kingdom of Portugal was founded in 1139 under Alfonso I, who called himself "King of Portugal and the Algarve". This makes Portugal one of the oldest nation states in the world. More buildings were destroyed in 1755 when a devastating earthquake struck the Algarve. The determination with which the region was rebuilt was second to none and it is for this reason that nearly all city centres are rebuilt in the 18th century style. In 1910 Portugal did away with the monarchy and proclaimed itself a republic. In 1932 Prime Minister António Salazar installed an authoritarian dictatorship with the help of the secret police or PIDE. Although the public treasury thrived, the people sunk into poverty. A revolt broke out on 25 April 1974. The people who had come out into the streets placed red carnations into the barrels of the rebel soldiers' guns – this was the peaceful almost bloodless coup that became known as the *"Carnation Revolution"*. It ended the dictatorship and led to Portugal joining the community of Western democracies. From the 1980s onwards, the Algarve began to turn into a cosmopolitan region par excellence.

A cosmopolitan region par excellence

With the rate of tourism increasing holiday establishments began to spring up unchecked along the coastline. Here the tourism buzz can be felt day and night in the

From 750
Christian quest to conquer the area (Reconquista)

1139
The Kingdom of Portugal is founded and is recognised by the Pope 30 years later

1249
The Algarve is finally conquered by the Christians. Henceforth the ruler calls himself "King of Portugal and the Algarve"

1395–1460
Prince Henry the Navigator as governor of the Algarve becomes the forefather of the "seafaring nation of Portugal" with the era of great discoveries starting in 1419

summer. However, the magic of the coast itself remains unspoilt and thankfully by now great care has been taken not to subject its natural beauty to exploitation. Strict conditions that are intended to prevent indiscriminate development have been introduced and non-intrusive tourism as in the form of the '"Via Algarviana" – a 300 km/186 miles inland hiking trail – and systematic recycling are indicative of the emergence of environmental consciousness.

The west coast *Costa Vicentina* is a traditional nature reserve. Many visitors regard this wilderness as the most impressive coastline in Europe. Here waves of colossal force batter the cliff walls, the surf spraying a hundred metres high on some days. The Algarve west coast and the hinterland lead their own quiet existence and are literally cut off from the bustling coastal zone by the A 22 motorway. Surrounded by *unspoilt nature* only very few people live in the Algarve hinterland now, mainly the elderly who live in remote houses or villages where time seems to stand still. Life there seems to be centred on hubs like Loulé, Silves or Monchique, while the surrounding administrative districts are becoming more sparsely populated. Young people have been leaving to work in the coastal cities to enjoy a more modern lifestyle – that is, if they find work, as secure jobs are far from guaranteed in crisis-ridden Portugal. But there are also counter currents – away from the hectic life towards deceleration, and to the country.

Tourists discover the tranquil hinterland

There, eco-tourism is starting to make a name for itself. Tourists are discovering the enchanting, tranquil and mountainous hinterland and the untarnished west coast. These areas are best explored on foot or by bicycle. The rewards are constant – pure, unspoilt nature at its best. The flora and fauna are rich and diverse, nature lovers and birdwatchers will be impressed by the many birds they will come across in the protected breeding places along the lagoons and cliffs – from flamingos to herons, from storks to stints.

With more than 3,000 hours of sunlight in a year, the Algarve is picture-perfect on most days and lives up to the promise of an ideal holiday: *heavenly beaches*, azure skies, clear waters. Many attractions and events – especially in the summer – are additional magnets for all generations. Optimal conditions for surfers, sailors and

1498
The sea route to India is opened, Brazil is discovered in 1500 – Portugal becomes a global empire

1580
Portugal loses its independence to Spain...

1640
...and regains it after a revolt but its global empire has already begun to crumble

1755
Severe earthquake strikes Portugal and the Algarve followed by concerted reconstruction of destroyed towns. In 1756, Faro becomes the Algarve's capital

1910
Proclamation of the republic

divers allow them to pursue their hobbies all year round. Not to mention the *golfers*! The Algarve's mild climate and the golf courses draw them here from all over the world. They have the opportunity to play a round of golf at close on 40 venues that have been seamlessly integrated into nature. Exclusive holiday establishments and

Blooming Algarve: Jacaranda trees at the foot of the cathedral and castle in Silves

golf courses have opened in Tavira, Vilamoura, Quinta du Lago, Carvoeiro, Alvor and Lagos. These fine resorts are almost like self-contained islands. On the whole, life in the Algarve is permeated by all aspects of a tourism orientated

Tee off on one of the 40 golf courses

existence. What always comes across is a hospitality that is very refreshing. At times things may take a little longer than elsewhere but you will always experience the true Algarve and its friendliness when out shopping, walking, at the market, at the café or simply asking for directions. It is almost as though the harmony of nature is mirrored by its people. And their friendly nature has always defied every crisis..

1928
Finance Minister António Salazar becomes Prime Minister and dictator in 1932

1974
The "Carnation Revolution" puts an end to the Salazar dictatorship

1986
Portugal joins the EU and the Euro is introduced in 2002

2012–2014
Portugal is handed 78 billion euros from the euro rescue package

2015/16
State debt remains high with continuing welfare cutbacks

WHAT'S HOT

1 Action & Reflection

Riding the wave Harmonising body and soul and enjoying the Algarve's beauty while surfing: this mixture of yoga and surfing is perfect, since yoga helps you get a firm grip on the surfboard. If an energy boost is what you need to keep you going, opt for a vegetarian lunch on the beach at *Algarve Yoga (Quinta das Pedras | Monte Velho | www.algar veyoga.com).* The *Algarve Surf & Yoga Retreat Portugal (Aljezur | www.surfalgarve.com)* offers yoga in the morning and in the evenings – for a good board feeling.

Living Green

2

Unusual ⓥ Spend the night in a luxury tepee, a safari tent or a yurt at the *Eco-Retreat Tipi Algarve (Monte João Afonso | south of Monchique | www.tipi algarve.com) (photo)* and enjoy their home-grown organic food. Sleep in a gypsy caravan or converted fire engine: The *Ecolodge Brejeira (eco-lodgebrejeira. com | Silves)* is alternative in every way and is sun and wind powered in its entirety. Water comes from their own source.

Fado appetizer

3

Short concerts Portugal is witnessing a revival of its traditional blues music, fado, thanks to the committed efforts of some such as the cultural association in Tavira *Fado com História (Rua Damião Augusto de Brito Vasconcelos 4 | fadocomhistoria.wix.com/fado).* This association organises programs of short fado concerts steeped in atmosphere from Monday to Saturday with tickets to be had from just 5 euros. Fado professionals also perform at the *Café O Cais (Rua José Estêvão 2 | Silves).*

Rustic Bliss

Tried and trusted Traditional country estates take holidaymakers to bygone times. During their restoration great care was taken to retain their historical charm using traditional building methods and rustic elements. The trademark of the *Vila Valverde Design Country Hotel (Estrada da Praia da Luz | Valverde | Lagos | www.vilavalverde.com) (photo)* is an eclectic mix of old and new. The 19th century estate has been completely updated, with contemporary glass walls contrasted with traditional rustic stone. For unrivalled romanticism stay at the *Vivenda Miranda (Porto Mós | Lagos | www.vivendamiranda.com)*, a 300 year old villa converted into a boutique hotel above the cliffs of Porto Mós. The *Pousada de Tavira – Convento da Graça (Rua D. Paio Peres Correia | Tavira | www.pousadas.pt)* is a former 16th century convent that has been lovingly restored and is now a hotel with contemporary décor.

Creative Algarve

Tradition, re-invented The Algarve is a region steeped in culture and tradition. The association *Loulé Criativo (www.loulecriativo.pt)* in Loulé was founded to revive traditional Portuguese arts and crafts: here you can learn how to weave baskets, prepare specialty dishes from the Algarve and decorate tiles. Cork is indigenous to the Algarve. More recently this renewable raw material is being used to create distinctive fashion accessories. The *Caleidoscópio (Rua 25 Abril 6 | Alvor)* boutique sells bags, belts and caps all made from cork. Take the cork route, the *Rota da cortiça (www.rotadacortica.pt)*, and visit cork groves and a modern-day cork factory as well as learning about traditional production methods.

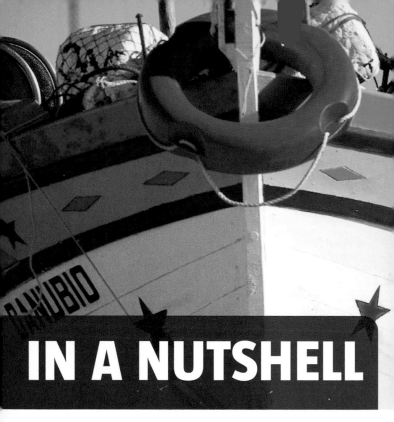

IN A NUTSHELL

A ZULEJOS

The term (pronounced: a-zoo-lay-shush) comes from the Arabic: *al-zulij* means "small stone". Decorative glazed ceramic tile art has its origins in Roman mosaics. The religious imagery depicts biblical scenes and saints, and there are some churches in the Algarve that are adorned with tiles. Particularly splendid examples include the Igreja de São Lourenço on the edge of Almancil, the Igreja de Santo António in Lagos and the Ermida de Nossa Senhora da Conceição in Loulé. In a domestic context the images are mainly of animals, so-called *motivo solteiro*, but there are also battle scenes and traditional life (e.g. agriculture and viticulture). In the course of reconstruction after the earth-quake in 1755, industrial tile production was necessitated in many of the cities. This was its triumph – *azulejos* have developed into Portugal's most appealing art form.

B EACHES

Superb beaches are the hallmark of the Algarve and justifiably so! To compile a list of its most beautiful beaches would be doing it an injustice, because every beach offers something special, be it in the flat sandy Algarve or beneath the Barlavento cliffs and on the islands in the nature reserve Ria Formosa. Take your pick. You can choose a small secluded beach or one that is 10 km/6 miles long. The sand is fine golden white with easy access into the water (not everywhere,

From seafarers and their aspirations: What you need to know about the nature, people and culture of the Algarve

of course). The Atlantic often reveals its wilder side at the Costa Vicentina, to the delight of surfers. Yet the enormous, sometimes metre-high tidal range, i.e. the difference between the high and low tides, needs to be respected in this region: always consult the tide times before you head out.

CHIMNEYS

They are a unique feature of the Algarve, ornately decorated house chimneys in a myriad of shapes. Some are round, others oblong, some used for the oven to bake bread, others for an open fireplace. Some are plain and others have been decorated so lovingly that they could be mistaken for signs put up by the owners. It is hardly surprising that these distinctive chimneys have become an emblem of sorts for the Algarve. Historians recognise disguised minarets in them which goes back to when the region was claimed back from the Moors and Christianity was enforced with a vengeance.

CORK

The Algarve hinterland is a region of abundant cork oak groves. Cork bark has 13 million cells per square inch, making it an extremely light, elastic and watertight material. Once the 3–5 cm thick bark layer has been peeled off the trunk, the number of the previous harvest year is painted on to it. It takes nine years for the

Church steeple? Minaret? No: a traditional Algarve chimney!

layer to grow back and this will determine when it is ready to be harvested once again. A "6" would mean that it was peeled in 2016 and is next due for harvest in 2025. Portugal is the world's biggest exporter of cork. Cork has a wide variety of uses, the bark is used for things like cork stoppers and floor tiles, while the cork resin is used as an insulation material in items such as shoe soles. Increasingly more artisans are using cork in their creations. Cork leather has also become fashionable and is used to make bags and wallets as well as more unusual items such as ties, hats and caps. Today you can even find wedding dresses made from cork leather.

ENVIRONMENT

Environmental awareness is on the increase in Portugal, with the media, international influences and educators playing a significant role not only in teaching greater ecological awareness but also practising it with excursions, workshops and projects such as beach clean-ups or the reforestation of burnt forests. Increasingly politicians from all the parties have had to bow to the pressure of integrating "green" concepts into their policies. Several organisations are making a strong case for the environment, achieving great success with their protests, ensuring that the old style of corrupt lobbying is no longer common practice. If local authorities and politicians abide by the laws they have drawn up themselves, this will be seen as progress in itself.

FAUNA

The Algarve's Atlantic Ocean is rich in marine life thanks to the perfect combination of the warm, mild Gulf Stream current and cooler water, making it home to a great variety of species. Divers can look forward to spotting sea bass, moray eels, monkfish and sea bream.

The cork oak forests are home to a rich diversity of animals including plenty of wild boar. As they are extremely timid animals you'd be very lucky to spot one during the day. You may also see Stone Martens, Egyptian mongoose or the increasingly rare genet.

The birdlife is also remarkably diverse. The Algarve – especially the food rich lagoons of the Ria Formosa – is the pit stop for their annual migration to and from Africa. There are an abundance of waders and waterfowl like flamingos, heron and storks. Vultures sometimes flock in from Morocco for a fleeting visit and there are a variety of different species of eagles resident inland. Children will love spotting chameleons or finding little seahorses in the shallows or the turtles that can be found in rivers such as the Ribeira de Odelouca. Beware of the spider fish *peixe aranha*. It buries itself in the sand and if you happen to step on to its venomous spikes, the pain and swelling can be quite severe. It is advisable to seek medical attention immediately! You may come across scorpions and sand vipers in the Sotavento but they are rare. Their sting or bite is not dangerous, but it is best to see a doctor.

FISHING

Today the once formidable fishing industry is no longer on a par with the past, when several port cities were home to one fish factory after another all canning tuna and sardines. Sardines are still the all-time favourite, followed by squid and octopus. The list of the most eaten seafood includes horse mackerel *(carapau)*, tuna, dried cod *(bacalhau)*, Cherne or stone bass and prawns *(gambas)*. The Portuguese consume an impressive amount of fish, far above the international average – no wonder when you live so close to the source and you can enjoy fresh fish straight from the barbecue. Every now and again conflicts arise about fishing quotas or the activities of their encroaching Spanish neighbours. Fishing quotas are redefined annually and show a strong downward trend. Stocks of some fish species remain constant while others, not least some species of tuna, are facing extinction. Growing numbers of farmed fish are being consumed, particularly sea bream and sea bass.

Incidentally, the bright colours of the fishing boats may make them aesthetically pleasing but the real reason for this is safety – it makes them more visible in the fog.

LITERATURE

From the 12th century onwards the development of literature went hand in hand with the formation of a national identity and a single Portuguese language. In the early 16th century Luís de Camões became the country's national poet with his tribute to its maritime discoveries. In the 20th century, José Maria Eça de Queiroz, then Fernando Pessoa and finally the 1998 Nobel Prize winner José Saramago (1922–2010) all gained international standing. In contemporary literature, Lídia Jorge, born in the Algarve in 1946, is regarded as Portugal's most respected author. In her works, she paints a realistic picture of contemporary society.

MOORS

In 711 Arab tribes crossed the Strait of Gibraltar and conquered most of the Iberian Peninsula. An advanced civilisation sprung up with academies for medicine, mathematics and astronomy. In the 12th century the knight Afonso Henriques succeeded in garnering support against the Moors. One Saracen castle after another was overpowered and he was victorious against the Moors. In 1179 Pope Alexander II recognised the conquered territory a kingdom – an independent Portugal came into being. The Algarve however remained Moor territory until the middle of the 13th century when Faro fell into the hands of the Crusaders. The regent Afonso Henriques now wore the crown as "King of Portugal and the Algarve".

The legacy of an era that lasted almost half a millennium is clearly visible to this day. It is manifested in the faces of Portugal's people, their stoic attitude to life, in the country's cuisine and in the tolerance –

even religious – which was characteristic of the Moors. Last but not least: many place names in the Algarve have Arabic roots – all those beginning with "Al" or "Gua", like Aljezur and Alcoutim as well as the Rio Guadiana.

MUSIC

Fado is the Portuguese blues. It was born in the poor neighbourhoods of Lisbon in the 19th century and gradually became a socially acceptable music genre.

Many bars in the Algarve organise live acts playing fado, with its soulful and emotional singing voices accompanied by poignant guitar rhythms. Fado is continuously re-inventing itself, incorporating classical elements, rock and jazz as well as Arabic, African and Brazilian influences.

To testify to the effect nostalgic fado has had on music in Portugal, this music genre was inscribed in the Unesco intangible cultural heritage list in 2011. The modern-day goddesses of fado still grace their occasional presence at concerts held in the Algarve including Mariza, Ana Moura and Cristina Branco. The MED festival, the so-called world music festival, is well worth a visit which is held every year in Loulé at the end of June. At live music gigs in bars around the Algarve (e.g. in Faro, Albufeira and Lagos) you can also witness the ever-changing pop and rock scene in the south of Portugal.

SEAFARERS

In 1415 at the age of 19, Prince Henry the Navigator *(Infante D. Henrique)* proved himself in the conquest of Ceuta in Morocco and as his reward, was accorded two positions: He became head of the wealthiest Portuguese order, the Order of Christ, and governor of the Algarve. In 1420 the prince made Lagos his official seat, where he surrounded himself with masters of mathematics, astronomy and cartography. He developed navigation, built instruments, and had land and ocean charts drawn up. He built the first caravels by combining the useful features from the North Sea and Mediterranean ships into one design – rudder in the hull, triangular sails and low draught. Henry's new captains eagerly set sail and already in 1419 João Zarco landed in Madeira. In 1434 Gil Eanes circumnavigated the Cape of Bojador in the Canary Islands. The Azores were discovered next, followed by the Gold Coast of Africa. The colonial system blossomed during Prince Henry's reign and with it came the exploitation of slaves – a different aspect of Portugal's "Golden Age". The first official slave market made its appearance in Lagos in 1444. What started off with 50 slaves soon escalated to more than 100,000 several years on. By the time the slave trade had officially ended in the 19th century, more than 20 million African people had been shipped off to the other side of the Atlantic to the American continent – predominantly by British, Dutch and French slave traders.

By the time Prince Henry died in Sagres in 1460, he had changed the face of the Portuguese world and the success story would continue. In 1487 Bartolomeu Diaz sailed around the Cape of Good Hope. Vasco da Gama completed the sea route to India in 1497–98. The profit from the sale of one consignment of spices that he brought back made his expedition worthwhile many times over. The outcome was that Lisbon would replace Venice as the centre of the spice trade and Portugal became a colonial power.

TIMES OF CRISIS

Collapse of the construction industry, tax increases, funds from the EU rescue package, severe welfare cutbacks – Portugal has recently gone through hard times, the consequences of which are still being felt. Living standards have dropped to a low point and the Portuguese are being forced to survive on modest means. Due to a lack of investors, new buildings in the Algarve have transformed overnight into ruins while other properties are still waiting for prospective buyers. Nobody's job is even safe, never mind the idea of wage increases for average employees. Many people fear for their livelihood and have been forced into finding alternative ways of making an income, something which the Portuguese have had practise in throughout their history. Besides the black market and under-the-counter sales, Portugal has also witnessed a resurgence in bartering which works as follows: The dentist repairs a tooth in exchange for a kilo of goose barnacles or a freshly caught fish. A car can also be repaired on a reciprocal exchange basis. In fact, the bartering of goods knows no boundaries. The only loser in this system is the state who cannot be relied on anyway.

VEGETATION

Hardy plants like umbrella pines and fig trees that are salt and wind-tolerant thrive along the shoreline. In the hinterland entire hills are covered in rock rose bushes *(cistus)*. On hot summer days their pink and white blossoms envelop the area with their resinous scent. Found among the Algarve's indigenous vegetation are laurels, common gorse, tree heath, strawberry trees and cork oak trees. Subtropical plants thrive in all their glory both along the coastline and in the coastal mountains or *serras*.

In the latter you will be able to pick plenty of tasty edible mushrooms. If it is chanterelles you are after, winter is the time to look for them among the cork oak trees. The entire coastline is resplendent with the scent of lavender, mint, oregano, sage, rosemary and thyme. They all thrive in the scrubland vegetation found here, equalled only by places such as the Azores, the Canary Islands, Cape Verde and Madeira. The orange and lemon groves in the belt between the coastal zone and coastal mountains can be traced back to the Moors, as can the small almond tree plantations.

Pink flamingos are abundant at the mouth of the Rio Guadiana

FOOD & DRINK

Going out for a meal is one of the greatest delights the Algarve has to offer, as you can still have an excellent meal in unpretentious restaurants – and at excellent prices. For only 15 euros you will be able to feast on fish specialities that would certainly cost you far more at home – if they are served there at all.

A number of local restaurants – especially in the vicinity of Vilamoura and Albufeira – serve French, Italian, Indian or Chinese cuisine. For the most part though, the restaurants found in the Algarve are fortunately typical of the region. The gastronomy scene is subject to fluctuation and not every restaurant can keep its head above water – there is a staggering 23.25 percent VAT on food and drink in Portugal.

Most restaurants offer a reasonably priced set tourist menu for between 10 and 15 euros which sometimes includes a beverage and an espresso. Many restaurants also offer an inexpensive *prato do dia*. This daily special is changed every day so you will be guaranteed the freshest fish or meat. Some simple restaurants may even give you the option of ordering INSIDER TIP *meia dose*, a half portion, which in reality equates to 70 % of a normal portion which also applies to the price. In the past, vegetarians may have had a hard time, but chefs are recognising the trend and are now adding vegetarian meals to their menus.

Seafood is the all-time favourite choice. This becomes obvious when you visit a

Grilled, fried, stewed or on a skewer: fish and seafood are at the top of the culinary list

fish market. The freshly caught selection spread out on tables is an impressive sight. Just as impressive is the knowledge with which the locals select their fish. You can take full advantage of this **large variety of fish and shellfish** in most restaurants, especially if you dare try the typical Algarve specialities.

What the wok is to the Chinese, the ● *cataplana* is to any Algarve local: A sealed cooking utensil (that vaguely resembles a flying saucer) is used to steam whatever ingredients are on hand at

the time, be it vegetables, fish, shellfish, meat or a few tasty slivers of *chouriço*. Fish is often just simply prepared on the grill. The slow heat brings out amazingly intense flavours and tastes. The basic principle of nouvelle cuisine is fulfilled to the utmost here with fresh top quality ingredients. Meat, mostly pork and chicken, is also served grilled. Oven dishes are called *estufado* and best lend themselves to kid goat, lamb and eel. *Feijoadas* are bean stews, often prepared with a Brazilian influence and are always hearty,

LOCAL SPECIALITIES

amêijoas – clams, usually cooked in white wine with plenty of garlic and coriander

arroz de marisco – seafood rice platter with crabs, mussels, clams, cockles, scampi and langoustine

bacalhau – dried cod prepared several ways – Portugal's national dish served *à brás* (with eggs), *com natas* (in cream, onions and garlic) or *cozido* (boiled)

bifanas – thin pork slices well fried in garlic and served in a bread roll

bife – *de atum* (tuna), *de novilho* (veal) or *de porco* (pork) steaks

carne à alentejana – stew of marinated pork, clams and coriander served with e. g. French fries

choco – squid grilled or fried or in a bean stew *(feijoada com chocos)* – the ink is often not removed with the smaller ones

ozido à portuguesa – hearty meat platter with plenty of cabbage

frango – different variations of grilled chicken (photo left) – *piri-piri* means extra hot

lulas – calamari (squid) served in tomato sauce or stuffed with ham *(recheadas)*

peixe espada – usually grilled silver or black scabbard fish – a delicate deep sea fish from the Madeira archipelago

peixe espadarte – swordfish or sawfish generally grilled on a coal fire or fried

pescada – fried or grilled seafood usually served with salad and rice or potatoes on the side

polvo – octopus – delicious in a *salada de polvo*

risol de camarão – fried shrimp turnovers

sapateira – crab is cheaper than lobsters or langoustines

sardinhas grelhadas – grilled sardines (photo right)

sopa à alentejana – a hearty soup with whole cloves of garlic, egg, bread and plenty of fresh coriander

even when delicate ingredients such as *búzios* (snails) or *chocos* (squid) are added.

The Algarve is responsible for almost the entire country's yield of mussel, clam and cockle harvest and wherever you go, you can expect to be served *mexilhões* (mussels), *amêijoas* (clams) or *berbigões* (cockles), also crab-like creatures called **INSIDER TIP** *perceves* (barnacles).

Whether you have them as a starter, or as a special treat, they go exceptionally well with a beer or a cold **vinho verde**. The fact that they come from perfectly clean water makes them even more sought after. The **clams, mussels and cockles** thrive in the Ria Formosa and the Ria de Alvor. *Perceves* grow along the cliffs of the west coast. Due to the constant battering by the waves and water, harvesting them is very risky, wich explains the high prices.

The desserts will also have you waxing lyrical. A *pudim flan* is delicate and delicious and there are also other *doce da casa* (Algarve-style desserts) to tempt you – tantalising delicacies made from whipped egg whites and almonds, figs, citrus fruits, cream and other sweet ingredients.

Most restaurants serve house wines *(vinho de casa)*, which are good and affordable. It is however still worth taking a look at the wine list. You are likely to find only Portuguese wines on the wine list and there is a reason for this. Wine connoisseurs rate these wines highly and guard this fact as their best kept secret. The most well known vineyards are found in Douro, Dão, Bairrada, Ribatejo, Terra do Sado and Alentejo.

Viticulture in the Algarve, which was neglected over a long time, has experienced a true resurgence in the past few years. Some *adegas* (wine cellars) open their doors to visitors to show them how their wine is produced. The Mediterranean climate, the soil quality and traditional cultivation methods and the salt content in the air are all conducive to the production of a wine that has very little acidity, a high alcohol content and special character. Bottle prices for decent, good-quality wines (white, rosé or red) start from 3–4 euros.

Port, the famed fortified wine from the north of the country, has a special role. A number of good wines or blends fro the Douro valley are expertly enriched with brandy which gives it its characteristic taste. Another speciality is *vinho verde* (green wine), which is a young sparkling wine low in alcohol that should be served well chilled.

After a meal – or at any other time of the day – a *bica* or strong espresso is highly recommended. After a meal, *medronho* – the schnapps made from the strawberry tree – or a brandy is the order of the day. When touring inland, ask for a *bica com cheirinho* and you will be served an espresso with a shot of brandy or *medronho*.

Sun, beach and ice-cold drinks from the snack bar: that's holiday!

SHOPPING

Shopping in the Algarve can be a sheer joy if you are on the lookout for an unexpected gem and if you avoid the many conventional souvenir shops. These tend to sell the very colourful ceramic items manufactured in northern Portugal or even "Made in China". If you take the time to shop properly for typical Algarve things, you will come across beautiful items made from cork, leather, olive wood; hand-painted ceramics, basketwork and wooden spoons; excellent cooking oils and spiced vinegar and homemade liqueurs and spirits. Souvenir shops can be found in all the big towns but for the really good ones head inland.

CERAMICS & POTTERY

This popular commercial art can be found in countless variations, be it as vases, plates (often with beautiful illustrations) and bowls, or as *azulejos* (decorative glazed ceramic tiles) or as souvenirs such as the "rooster of Barcelos", the national symbol of Portugal, which originated from a legend. Sardines made out of ceramics are a pretty wall decoration with a difference. You can find pottery shops in Loulé , for example, and in Loulé's market hall.

Pottery workshops that produce typically Portuguese products – such as hand painted plates, cups, bowls and vases – can be found alongside the N125, with the pottery workshops in Porches as the most well known. Today, modern designs are mingling with traditional shapes and colours.

CORK & BASKETRY

The bark of the cork oak trees is transformed into cork leather or fabric in a complex manufacturing process to be then used to produce unusual goods that are well suited to souvenirs such as glasses cases and wallets. If you stroke the material, you'll notice how silky smooth it feels. Aditionally there are watches, bags, picture frames and bowls.

Straw and willow are used for the production of a whole range of goods, not only baskets but also small pretty bottle covers with handles.

METAL WARE & JEWELLERY

Choose lamps and lanterns fashioned from tin, copper Cataplana pans, vases and plates from pewter or balustrades and chimney accessories from iron.

Ceramics, cork, glazed fruit: there's an excellent selection of special souvenirs

There are countless good jewellers in the Algarve because here tradition still holds that if a woman comes into money she invests it in jewellery. The gold is ruddier and darker than you may now it from back home.

SWEET & SAVOURY

All kinds of *doces*: if you can resist the urge to eat them right away, they make a nice souvenir. Moorish influence still prevails with lots of figs, almonds, eggs, honey and fresh or glazed fruit. An extensive variety can be found in all *pastelarias* (confectionary shops) – and the Algarve has a lot of them. A sweet but strong souvenir is carob liquor.

Sea salt, the "white gold", is quarried, for instance, near Castro Marim. The production of INSIDERTIP *flor do sal* or salt flower (the hand-harvested premium layer) is very complex; some shops sell it in small packets. A new addition to the range of products is liquid salt *(sal liqui-do)* with a high content of magnesium available in spray bottles.

WOOD & LEATHER

There are many arts and crafts shops that sell spoons, mortars and pestle, spice grinders, pendants and small boards, all made from old olive wood. You can also find nice things on markets. The popular Roman collapsible "folding chair" is probably only an option if you've come by car.

Some shoemakers still produce tailor-made leather shoes and boots in the traditional way. The regional markets carry a remarkably large selection of inexpensive shoes from northern Portugal.

THE BARLAVENTO

The Barlavento coast – with its distinctive cliffs – stretches from Sagres to Praia da Falésia in Albufeira. It is densely built up, with lots of small towns, villas, hotels and golf courses setting the scene. However, the shoreline remains largely untouched.

Dunes spread out from the estuaries of small rivers blending in with steep cliff walls that go on for kilometres. Over the millennia wind and weather have chiselled out bizarre rock sculptures, at times forming kilometres of beach, at others small coves and grottoes – idyllic spots to swim and sunbathe. With its enchanting gifts of nature and its clear turquoise water, the Algarve has won recognition as Europe's most beautiful coastline.

ALBUFEIRA

MAP INSIDE BACK COVER
(137 F6) *(Ø J7)* Once a fishing village, ★ Albufeira is nowadays famed for its beaches and wide-spread city centre making it the busiest tourist destination of the Algarve. This large municipality with its wide selection of hotels stretches far along the coast; the distance from the east to the west of Albufeira is surprisingly long.

Albufeira has become a major holiday resort popular with tourists hungry for a getaway. In winter some 40,000 people live here, during the summer holidays these numbers swell to over 300,000. Because of this the place is famous for its

An Eldorado for sun worshippers: beaches, bays, coves and bizarre rocks make up this superb coast

lively nightlife and party atmosphere. Even Lisbon's trendsetters and in-crowd flock to the local clubs to make their stylish presence felt at "the strip". This is why many call Albufeira the "St Tropez of the Algarve". Nice, atmospheric hang-outs can also be found around the modern marina a bit further to the west.

The city centre with its jumble of whitewashed houses is reminiscent of a Roman amphitheatre. Souvenir stalls make the already narrow, cobbled alleyways difficult to negotiate. Cafés, bars and restaurants go on forever, while street artists vie for a spot on the streets. Its proximity to the beach is what defines this city, but the best beaches like the Praia da Falésia are located far outside the eastern city gates. The further you head away from *Cais Herculano* on the one side and the area in the vicinity of the main square, the *Largo Engenheiro Duarte Pacheco*, and *Rua 5 de Outubro* on the other, the more you will leave behind the tourist rush, giving you a chance to enjoy the quieter charms of Albufeira. Especially if you take

Strolling through Albufeira's city centre

a stroll around the old *Cerro da Vila* area where neighbours grill their sardines on the side of the road, catch up on the latest gossip in front of their low porches and time tends to go by the old Portuguese way – wonderfully slowly.

SIGHTSEEING

❋ Steps take you to the remains of a castle which clarifies the Arabic place name: *Al-buhera* translates as "fortress at the sea". Located at the edge of the cliff top it once protected the flourishing harbour. This part of the old city, the *Cerro da Vila*, was destroyed by the 1755 earthquake. A fantastic view of the city's beaches and the impressive rocky coastline is to be had from the *Rua da Bateria*. In the *Travessa da Igreja Velha* you will see the arch of a mosque dating back to the Moors and in *Rua Henrique Calado* you will find the *Misericórdia Chapel* and what remains of the city's fortification.

FOOD & DRINK

LA CIGALE
Elegant beachfront restaurant specialising in fish, shellfish from a basin, and steaks. 4 km/2.5 miles to the east in *Olhos de Àgua*. *Tel. 2 89 50 16 37 | www.restauran telacigale.net | Expensive*

EVARISTO
Elegant restaurant right on Evaristo beach, next to Praia da Galé. Bright, spacious, modern design. In high season it is often frequented by VIPs, hence the higher prices. Dining here will always be a memorable experience. *Tel. 2 89 59 16 66 | www. evaristo.pt | Expensive*

A RUINA
It forms part of what was once the castle cistern and is located on the *Praia dos*

Pescadores. Enjoy freshly caught fish with excellent house wines on one of the four terraces and take in the spectacular view of the popular beach. *Tel. 2 89 51 20 94 | www.restaurante–ruina.com | Moderate*

UZONJ

Fine cuisine with a special touch and excellent value for money. The high ratings on respected online forums are no coincidence. *Estrada Santa Eulália | tel. 2 89 54 36 26 | Moderate*

SHOPPING

The alleyways in the *Rua 5 de Outubro* pedestrian zone are like an open air department store where plenty of odds and ends and things "made in China" are on display; you will also come across hawkers selling reasonably priced African ethnic arts and crafts. *The regional market is always held on the first and third Tuesday of the month, flea market on the second and third Saturday of the month*

BEACHES

City beaches: *Praia dos Pescadores* can be reached from *Cais Herculano, Praia do Penedo* is accessed through the beach tunnel and this is where most holidaymakers head for. East of the city: *Praia da Oura, Balaia, Maria Luísa* to *Olhos de Água* are all popular but there is a parking problem; behind the Sheraton Hotel stretches the beautiful *Praia da Falésia* with its many sections. Located west of the city are a selection of magnificent beaches in bays surrounded by cliffs: *Baleeira, São Rafael, Vigia, Castelo* all the way to ● *Praia da Galé.*

SPORTS & ACTIVITIES

Diverse boat trips set off from the marina to the west of Albufeira, a popular sailing route takes you west towards Carvoeiro. Catamaran tours available from *Algarve Charters (tel. 2 89 31 48 67 | www. algarvecharters.com).*

ENTERTAINMENT

KISS CLUB & DISCO
Popular clubbing hotspot in the city's nightlife scene. *During the season daily. 11pm–6am | approx. 15 euros | Rua Vasco da Gama*

CITY CENTRE
At night the Albufeira city centre also gets lively especially in the vicinity of the *Largo Duarte Pacheco* Square, where there is live music at *Harry's,* the *Rua dos Bares* and *Rua Cándido dos Reis.* Scandinavian

---

★ **Albufeira**
Holiday atmosphere, a lively-beaches and nightlife → **p. 32**

★ **Nossa Senhora da Rocha**
A cliff chapel built by fishermen → **p. 37**

★ **Lagos**
Harbour city with a rich history and lots of activity → **p. 39**

★ **Ponta da Piedade**
Bizarre rock formations: caves, arches, grottoes → **p. 40**

★ **Ferragudo**
Picturesque fishing village with Fort São João do Arade at the Arade mouth → **p. 50**

★ **Sagres**
Fishing village with a castle and sheltered beaches → **p. 51**

MARCO POLO HIGHLIGHTS

and English bars make for plenty of activity, as do a few Portuguese ones.

THE STRIP

The "Albufeira Strip" is actually the Avenida Dr. Francisco Sá Carneiro, the connecting road between the districts *Montechoro* and *Areias de São João*. The amusement strip is defined by fun and entertainment and has something for everyone – from pubs to clubs, from gays to heteros. People from many countries come together here; in the summer, party time starts around midnight. New bars open on and behind the strip all the time – explore everything there is to discover to your heart's content all the way through to sunrise.

WHERE TO STAY

BOA VISTA ☆

The hotel has a beautiful view across the bay from the edge of the cliffs and is still very centrally located. *85 rooms | Rua Samora Barros 20 | tel. 289589175 | www.hotelboavista.pt | Moderate*

EPIC SANA ●

Exclusively modern hotel; the sight of its immense foyer is enough to be impressed. The complex is spread over 8 hectares and a short footpath leads you outside the complex to the Falésia beach. The apartments with a separate pool area are a good option for families. The large indoor pool and fitness centre are open for guests 24x7, the spa (free admission between 12 pm and 3 pm, additional cost at other times) features a sauna, steam bath and a second indoor pool. *184 rooms and suites, 43 apartments | Pinhal do Concelho | Praia da Falésia | Olhos de Água | tel. 289104300 | www.algarve.epic.sana hotels.com | Expensive*

SHERATON ALGARVE

A hallmark of luxury set in extensive parkland above the *Praia da Falésia* with its own golf course. It belongs to the Pine Cliff Resort which offers additional accomodation. *248 rooms and suites | tel. 289500100 | www.sheratonalgarve. com | Expensive*

INFORMATION

POSTO DE TURISMO

Rua 5 de Outubro | tel. 289585279 | www. cm-albufeira.pt

WHERE TO GO

ALCANTARILHA (137 D5) (⌀ H6)

The cafés and shops in this charming town (population 2,300; 10 km/6 miles northwest on the N 125) have a serene feel. The walls of the Chapel of the Deceased in the village church are "decorated" with 1,500 human skulls.

ARMAÇÃO DE PÊRA (137 D6) (⌀ H7)

Hotels and apartment blocks have turned this town located 15 km/9 miles west of Albufeira into a tourist stronghold. Out of season it has a population of 7,000, which skyrockets to 80,000 in peak season. The coast has wide, sandy beaches, especially well suited to children. This is also the case at *Praia Grande* east of the *Ribeira de Alcantarilha* riverbed (access via Pêra). Behind the Praia Grande lies the *Lagoa dos Salgados*, a lake great for birdwatching. ☆ An all encompassing view of the area can be had from the harbour fort and in the evening the *Havana Bar (Rua Dr. José António dos Santos 11)* draws in its guests with its Latin American music, cool drinks and an excellent vibe. *Rocha da Palha (tel. 2 82 31 55 96 | restau ranterochadapalha.pt | Moderate)* is a beach restaurant (central section) popular for its cuisine and location. An absolute must are their Açorda and Cataplana dishes or the squid kebabs.

The *Vilalara Thalassa Resort (124 suites and apartments | Praia das Gaivotas | Alporchinhos | tel. 282 32 00 00 | www. vilalararesort.com | Expensive)* has a

GUIA (137 E5) (*⊞ J6*)

This town is on the N 125, 6 km/4 miles north of Albufeira and is known for its main tourist attraction: *Zoomarine* (see p. 114). Guia is also synonymous with *frango piri-piri*, the spicy barbecue chicken served in a number of its restaurants.

Nothing is set in stone: sand sculptures at the Fiesa festival

pretty beach west of Armação de Pêra and directly next to the resort *Vila Vita Parc.* The hotel is renowned for its thalasso therapy and spa centre.

FIESA (137 D6) (*⊞ H7*)

Near Pêra, 4 km/2.5 miles to the north, lies the site of an annual sand sculpture festival which draws international artists. There's a new theme every year, and it's always about man and nature. The resulting huge figures or whole landscapes are admired by people of all ages. *End of May–end of June daily 10am–10pm, end f June–mid-Sept daily 10am–midnight; d-Sept–Oct daily 10am– 8pm | admis- ᵒ euros | www.fiesa.org*

Looming large directly off the N 125 is ● *Algarve Shopping* (www.algarveshop ping.pt)*, a massive shopping mall with cinemas, dozens of shops, supermarkets and fast food restaurants. There is plenty of activity on a rainy day but even on other days the centre is a magnet for tourists and residents alike.

NOSSA SENHORA DA ROCHA ★ ☀ (137 D6) (*⊞ H7*)

2 km/1.2 miles west of Armação de Pêra is a striking pilgrim's chapel perched on a cliff that has sweeping views of the coastline. Fishermen built it in the 16th century. Pillars from the 6th–7th century are a Visigoth testimony to early

Christianity. The chapel is dedicated to the Virgin Mary, whose image can be seen holding a child through a large glass front in an altar; the glass front on her side is turned to face a picturesque portico.

At the foot of the cliffs there are invitingly beautiful beaches. This is the beginning of a part of the coast that remains unrivalled with its caves and rock formations, grottoes and arches. This section goes all the way to *Carvoeiro*. The cliff edge makes for an excellent hiking opportunity.

Moderate – Expensive), an authentic family-run Algarve restaurant. Its wine cellar is well-stacked and it offers a hearty cuisine with many meat dishes. Have a dessert of fig-or carob cake after that, and you'll be full-up and happy!

PRAIA DA FALÉSIA (138 B4) (*∭ K7*)

8 km/5 miles to the east is a beautiful sandy beach that is several kilometres long. The beach lies at the foot of a 30 m/798 ft high cliff which marks the point where

Nossa Senhora da Rocha – a small chapel in a great location

PADERNE (137 F4) (*∭ K7*)

You will spot it from the motorway: the Moorish hill fort *Castelo de Paderne*. At the entrance of the town, head in the direction of Fonte; drive beneath the motorway bridge and voila ... a charming piece of countryside alongside a stream, the Ribeira da Quarteira with its Roman bridge, watermill and picnic spots.

Between Albufeira and Paderne, at the town of *Mem Moniz*, lies *Veneza (closed Tue, closed Wed lunchtime | tel. 2 89 36 71 29 | www.restauranteveneza.com |*

the rocky part of the Algarve merges with the flat, sandy part. The Falésia cliff face does not consist of rock as such but of baked red sand that crumbles away easily so it is best not to lie directly beneath it! This expansive beach with its fine sand is the perfect playground for children. Access roads lead to the various sections but parking near these is limited in high season, as is space on the beach.

PRAIA OLHOS DE ÁGUA
(138 B4) (*∅ K7*)

Undersea spring waters gave this place not far to the east its name "eyes of water". Occasionally you may see the "eyes" caused by the bubbling freshwater. At high tide the beach becomes quite narrow.

LAGOS

MAP INSIDE BACK COVER
(135 E4–5) (*∅ E6–7*) Also known as the "Pearl of the Algarve" the beautiful city of ⭐ Lagos stretches across the western part of an elongated bay. The Greeks and Romans used it as a harbour, while at the end of the Middle Ages, Henry the Navigator made it his headquarters for his caravel sailing ships.

It is from here that the Portuguese marine journeys of discovery began and there are many reminders of the beginnings of this "golden epoch". However it was also here that the end of this epoch was heralded in when in 1578, the young King Sebastião had the misguided idea to fight Islam in Morocco. He set off with 20,000 soldiers. Only a few returned and without their king. Portugal subsequently became a Spanish province for 60 years and by the time it became independent once again, the English and Dutch had picked its colonial empire to pieces.

Over the years the city (population of 30,000) has been able to retain its unique charm, which is clearly discernible in the old city. In the historical centre within the city walls are a maze of alleyways with cafés, shops, bars and restaurants. But it is not only the romantics that are in their element in this city. The nightlife is hip, the nearby beaches are divine and the coast offers the best conditions for all kinds of water sport. The *Marina* provides additional activity because sailors use it as a pit stop ahead of the long "Columbus Voyage" to the Canaries or Cape Verde and then on to the Caribbean. For guests of the city, the Marina is the starting point for shorter boat trips – for example dolphin watching or to the Ponta da Piedade. The prominent status that Lagos once held for its maritime history is what the city is striving to rekindle – this time around with tourism and a great repertoire of cultural events.

SIGHTSEEING

CITY WALL

The wall and gateway that replaced that of the Moors in the 16th century remains

---

LOW BUDGET

Low-budget private rooms and basic hotels are rented as *alojamento local* however you cannot pay for this type of lodging with credit card.

The *Orange Terrace Hostel (Rua Padre Semedo Azevedo 24 | tel. 2 89 04 78 95 | www.orange-terrace. com)* in Albufeira offers private rooms as well as a cheaper sleeping alternative in a dorm. WiFi is free and its 🛰 roof terrace is an excellent spot to meet other guests.

● Some locals sell their garden produce directly in front of their houses or on the roadside. Oranges, mandarins, melons and more besides are sold in nets or crates. You'll soon learn to notice these private sellers all over the Algarve. A good and affordable way to buy fresh produce!

Henry the Navigator, ruling over the central square in Lagos

partly intact. The section between the Praça Infante Dom Henrique and the Forte Ponta da Bandeira is particularly rewarding; a monument in front of the wall is dedicated to Gil Eanes, one of the 15th century Portuguese navigators and explorers, who is believed to have been born in Lagos. A particularly picturesque place is the INSIDERTIP city wall gateway *Arco de São Gonçalo*.

This medieval *muralha* provides a compelling backdrop for the open-air *Auditório Municipal* at Largo Dr. Vasco Gracias, which makes for a very special atmosphere during summer concerts and festivals.

FORTE PONTA DA BANDEIRA

The harbour fort was built between 1680 and 1690 to keep pirates at bay. Behind it, the harbour canal flows into the sea. Its small *museum* displays the history of the fortress. It is where the coastal promenade Avenida dos Descobrimentos begins and where you can take a boat ride to

Ponta da Piedade. *Tue–Sun 10am–12.30pm and 2–5:30pm | admission 3 euros*

IGREJA DE SANTO ANTÓNIO/MUSEU MUNICIPAL

A strange combination: You can only enter the Igreja de Santo António through the municipal museum. This church in Lagos is an art historian highlight. After the earthquake the church was rebuilt in 1769. Its unimposing exterior belies its interior – a lavish showcase of Algarve baroque with some remarkable gilded carvings and *azulejos*. Extraordinary scenes grace the walls with smiling angels floating above hideous ogres and fighting knights. The adjacent *museum (Tue–Sun 10am–12:30pm and 2–5:30pm | admission 3 euros)*, houses an extremely interesting collection of model ships and archaeological findings as well as a paintings' gallery, weapons, porcelain figures, silver bowls, coins and sacred sculptures. *Rua General Alberto Carlos da Silveira*

MUSEU DE CERA DOS DESCOBRIMENTOS

Hidden in a corner of the marina, this wax figure museum dedicated to the Portuguese Discoveries ("Descobrimentos") traces history through the eyes of 22 wax figures including Prince Henry the Navigator, King Manuel I, Vasco da Gama and Magellan. This brief stroll through history is accompanied with sound effects. *March/Oct 10am–6pm, April/June/Sept 10am–7pm, July/Aug 10am–11pm, Nov–Feb 10am–5pm | admission 5 euros | Marina da Lagos | Edificio Astrolábio | www.museuceradescobrimentos.com*

PONTA DA PIEDADE ★ ⋇

The up to 40 m/130 ft high, jagged weathered rock face begins at *Praia*

Ana with its peculiar grottoes and caves, arches and towers and small tucked away beaches. The only way to reach these is by climbing down some very steep steps. This bizarre sculpture-like landscape stretches for about 1,600 m/1 mile as far as the *Ponta da Piedade* lighthouse. The best way to appreciate it is by taking a boat trip from Lagos.

PRAÇA INFANTE DOM HENRIQUE

On Lagos' rambling central square you'll meet the man who gave the square its name: Henrique, or Henry the Navigator, as a monument. The ruler is seated in a regal posture, looking towards the river and far away to the Meia Praia. In the direction of the river, a small play area with water foountains brightens the square. Several historically important buildings line the Praça: the former *governor's palace* (seat of the Algarve governors from the 14th century onwards), the *Arsenal* from the 17th century, adorned with coats of arms, and in a corner of the square a building with four arcade arches showing the former *slave market (Mercado de Escavros)*. This is where the first official sale of African slaves took place in 1444. It was the beginning of the European slave trade and colonial period, which took such a bitter course for the exploited – a dark chapter in history. The most prominent structure on the Praça is the baroque *Igreja Santa Maria*, still used as a parish church. It is woth taking a look inside; the church is freely accessible.

PUBLIC ART

How one reacts to it will of course depend on the individual: in Lagos public art is quite provocative. This is especially true or the statue of the young king, Dom ̇bastião in the central *Praça Gil Eanes* ne of Portugal's most significant rs, João Cutileiro.

ADEGA DA MARINA

Large, rustic restaurant close to the indoor market hall that serves good-quality grilled meat and seafood. *Av. dos Descobrimentos 35 | tel. 2 82 76 42 84 | Budget*

ADEGA SEBASTIÃO

A traditional favourite in the pedestrian zone with a comfortable outdoor seating area. Vegetarian meals also available. If you can't find a seat in Sebastião, you can choose from a wide selection of other restaurants around and about. *Rua 25 de Abril 20–22 | tel. 2 82 78 04 80 | www. restaurantedonsebastiao.com | Moderate*

DON TORO STEAK HOUSE

The Algarve also has its steakhouses and this is the best – located alongside the-

Mighty city walls: the harbour fort of Forte Ponta da Bandeira

Centro Cultural in Lagos – it only serves Angus beef and will draw you in with its relaxed atmosphere. *Rua Lançarote de Freitas 12 | tel. 2 82 76 72 34 | www.don toro.com | Moderate*

SHOPPING

The *indoor market hall (Av. dos Descobrimentos)* is well worth a visit; fish is sold on the ground floor with fruit and vegetables on the first floor.

BEACHES

Stretching out to the east of Lagos is the *Meia Praia* – this vast sandy beach goes on for kilometres behind the railway line (which don't obstruct any views) , curving all the way to the Ria de Alvor. Surfers, kite surfers and windsurfers alike love the surf that you get here. However in summer it does tend to become very windy in the afternoon. Directly alongside the harbour fort is where the beaches of the Ponta da Piedade begin, from *Praia Dona Ana* (a favourite and very busy because of its unique rocks) to *Praia do Camilo.* To the west of the Ponta da Piedade lies *Porto Mós*, a small bay surrounded by cliffs with a beautiful beach near to Luz. In *Luz* the beaches are wide and sandy and very popular. Beautiful, quiet beaches can be found further along the coast if you head in the direction of Sagres from Burgau.

SPORTS & ACTIVITIES

Heading towards the *marina,* a number of booths on the promenade sell tickets for boat trips to Ponta da Piedade.

Crystal clear water, golden sands, grandiose rocks of Praia do Camilo

Advertised as "grotto tours", the trip takes you into natural rock caves and caverns. *Seafaris (www.seafaris.net)* or *Bom Dia Boat Trips (www.bomdiaboattrips.com)* also organise dolphin watching tours.

ENTERTAINMENT

The live music bar INSIDERTIP *Stevie-Ray's (Rua Senhora da Graça 9 | stevie-rays. com)* near the Praça Infante Dom Henrique is the place to be for jazz and blues enthusiasts even in the off-season, starting late on Fri and Sat. The next nightlife hotspot is located not far away on the same road: the *Grand Café Music Room.* Popular meeting point in the pedestrian zone is the *Taberna de Lagos Cocktail & Gin Bar (Rua Dr. Joaquim Tello/ Rua 25 de Abril).*

WHERE TO STAY

ALBERGARIA MARINA RIO
Despite its location on the main city thoroughfare, the hotel is close to the marina and pedestrian zone making it ideal for those who don't want to walk far. *30 rooms | Av. dos Descobrimentos | tel. 2 82 78 08 30 | marinario.com | Moderate*

CASA DOS SONHOS ●
Located in the *Mata Nacional* nature reserve, surrounded by various species of pines to the north-west of Lagos in *Barão de São João (135 D4) (⫪ D6)* Palm garden with a round swimming pond, really beautiful. *5 apartments | tel. 2 82 68 80 61 | www.casa-dos-sonhos. com | Moderate*

MARINA CLUB LAGOS RESORT
At a close distance yet away from the bustling centre – this resort is slightly hidden at the marina; its studio apartments and suites are assembled around a large, attractive pool. *88 suites and apartments | Marina de Lagos | tel. 2 82 79 06 00 | www.marinaclub.pt | Moderate*

VILA GALÉ LAGOS
Attractive hotel complex, 400 m/1,300 ft behind the Meia Praia with a large outdoor pool landscape set in spacious gardens and two tennis courts (free use for guests). The hotel is especially recommended for its INSIDERTIP cheaper off-season prices *(Budget–Moderate)*, when the indoor pool, sauna and fitness centre are less busy. *306 rooms | Rua Sophia de Melo Breyner Andresen | tel. 2 82 77 14 00 | www.vilagale.com | Expensive*

POSTO DE TURISMO

Praça Gil Eanes | tel. 2 82 76 30 31 | www. cm-lagos.pt

BARRAGEM DA BRAVURA ⤴
(135 E2–3) (⑰ D–E5)

A large artificial lake surrounded by forested hills, 15 km/9 miles north of Lagos. Ideal for a picnic on the lakeshore or just for the panoramic views. From *Odiáxere* take a drive along the charming route to the lake among eucalyptus trees, pines and gorse.

BOCA DO RIO (134 C5) (⑰ C–D7)

A small harbour built by the Romans at the mouth of a small river 15 km/9 miles west of Lagos. Above it are the ruins of a fort dating back to the 16th century.

BURGAU (135 D5) (⑰ D7)

This authentic fishing village (population of 700) 10 km/6 miles west of Lagos is popular for its beaches and beach pubs. At the village entrance a pretty road bends to the right to Boca do Rio and Salema. The INSIDERTIP *Quinta do Mar (5 rooms and 3 apartments| Sítio Cama da Vaca | Tel. 2 82 69 73 23 | www.quintamarluz. com | Moderate)*, a romantic and rustic establishment between Praia da Luz and Burgau, comes highly recommended and it has no less than three swimming pools.

LUZ (135 D5) (⑰ D7)

This welcoming beach and holiday resort (3,500 inhabitants) situated between Lagos and Burgau is extremely popular. And rightly so. The town gradually extends down the hillside to its beaches at the bottom; the restaurant *Fortaleza da Luz (Rua Igreja 3 | tel. 2 82 78 99 26 | Moderate)* close to the church is a good eating option. You can also enjoy a pleasant stroll below the church along the INSIDERTIP promenade prettily decorated with lanterns and palm trees to the town's main beach. Luz has many private apartment complexes and other types of accommodation such as the *Luz Beach Apartments (30 apartments| Praia da Luz | tel. 2 82 79 26 77 | www.luz beachapartments.com | Moderate)* close to the beach.

SALEMA (134 C5) (⑰ C7)

This coastal village is located 17 km/10.5 miles west of Lagos, it borders a fantastic beach that stretches between to rocky crags in a graceful arc. Behind the beach you'll find a small restaurant zone. For a nice spot with beach views, go to ⤴ *Restaurante Boia (Rua dos Pescadores 101 | tel. 2 82 69 53 82 | www. boiabar.com | Moderate)*.

PORTIMÃO

(136 B5) (⑰ F6) ⤴ Located on the coast at the mouth of the Rio Arade, Portimão (population of 45,000) boomed in the Nineties. Despite the many featureless new buildings, it succeeded in retaining its own – somewhat sombre – atmosphere.

This can be ascribed to the fishing boats, which chug past the city centre on the Rio Arade to the river harbour. The anchorage is well protected from wind and waves. Now the second-largest fishing harbour in the Algarve, it was also used by the Carthaginians and Romans (they called it "portus magnus" from which Portimão was derived) and later by the Moors. With its esplanades, palm trees, yac~~ marina, pier for cruise ships, cafés ~~ riverside promenade – the *Cais Vas~~*

Gama – the town has a hint of the exotic. A visit to Portimão should focus around this harbour area (signposted as "Zona Ribeirinha"); otherwise the town appears slightly confusing. Portimão is the shopping hub of the western Algarve. In August holidaymakers pour in for the famous *Festival da Sardinha*.

SIGHTSEEING

JESUIT COLLEGE
An imposing building, built between 1660 and 1707 with simple, clear lines. It includes a church, dormitories and lecture rooms. As with all Jesuit buildings in Portugal, the college was nationalised in 1834. Unfortunately it is not open to the public.

MUSEU DE PORTIMÃO ●
A former fish canning factory was converted into a museum that has managed to retain the building's architectural interest. The exhibition tells the history of the region's fishing, canning industry and ship building heritage. The climb down to the Roman cistern is particularly interesting. As the information boards are all in Portuguese, ask for the English-language brochure at the museum entrance. Also features special exhibitions. *Mid-July–Aug Tue 7:30pm–11pm, Wed–Sun 3–11pm, at other times Tue 2:30–6pm, Wed–Sun 10am–6pm | admission 3 euros*

FOOD & DRINK

A CASA DA ISABEL
A tiny café rich in tradition with a decorative façade – in the pedestrian zone. *Rua Direita 61 | tel. 2 82 48 43 15 | www.acasa daisabel.com | Budget*

CASA INGLESA
Founded in 1922, the traditional café in Portimão next to the harbour promenade attracts guests with its large terraces and hearty meals. *Praça Manuel Teixeira 2 | tel. 2 82 41 62 90 | Moderate*

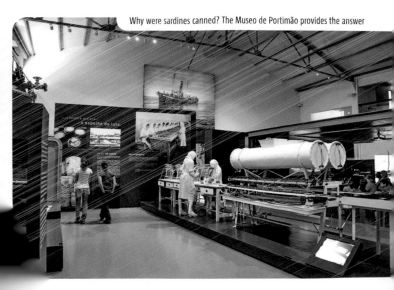

Why were sardines canned? The Museo de Portimão provides the answer

DONA BARCA

The heat is on in this restaurant located under the old Arade bridge – grilled fresh fish served daily! *Largo da Barca | tel. 282 48 41 89 | Moderate*

O MANÉ

Escalopes done on the BBQ as well as meat and seafood. The barbecued fish is the real favourite here though..

streets. At the *Parque de Feiras e Exposições* there's a regional market on the first Monday of the month, a flea market on the first and third Sunday of the month.

The *Aqua Portimão* is a massive shopping centre with more than 130 shops, cinemas, restaurants, a large supermarket and everything that you need. It is on the access road into Portimão and it is hard to miss.

In the restaurants – such as here in the Dona Barca – children are always welcome

Closed Sun | Largo Doutor Bastos 1 | tel. 282 42 34 96 | Budget–Moderate

TABERNA DA MARÉ

In a small street a few steps from Largo Doutor Bastos. Its speciality is squid but also serves fish and meat straight from the BBQ and seafood. *Closed Mon | Travessa da Barca 9 | tel. 282 41 46 14 | tabernadamare.pai.pt | Budget–Moderate*

SHOPPING

Countless shops are found in the pedestrian precinct *Rua do Comércio* and its side

BEACHES

The Praias on both sides of the mouth of the Rio Arade have fine golden sand, are expansive and are protected from waves. The ● *Praia da Rocha* beach is one of Portugal's most well known and the flagship of the Algarve. Wooden pathways have been laid out along the entire beach; higher above, Praia da Rocha is built-up all over. To the west are smaller bays with magnificent beaches: *Praia do Três Castelos, Praia do Amado* and *Praia dos Careanos,* followed by the ever ular *Praia do Vau* and *Praia do A*

You reach the next beach, *Praia do Caniço,* by taking the lift that has been built into the rock (at the Prainha resort). During low tide you can go on foot to the neighbouring *Praia dos Três Irmãos* that extends into the vast *Alvor* – a dune beach that goes on for kilometres.

From Ferragudo to Carvoeiro and then on to Benagil you will find one beautiful beach after another: *Praia Grande* in front of the pier is good for water sports, *Pintadinho* is next to it, *Marinha* is a cove beach under rocky outcrops and can be reached via stairs, *Benagil* is a sunny piece of paradise, *Carvalho* can be reached from Clube Atlântico via stairs and tunnel, *Centianes* becomes very narrow during high tide, while *Paraíso* has interesting rocks. The limited parking spaces near the beaches are always a problem.

SPORTS & ACTIVITIES

Take a boat ride up the rugged coastline to Armação de Pêra, Lagos, or up the Arade river as far as Silves. A trip on the mock pirate ship, the *Santa Bernarda (tel. 2 82 42 27 91 | www.santa-bernarda.com)*, is particularly pleasant. Tickets can be booked in hotels or on the *Cais Vasco da Gama.*

The *Divers Cove* in *Carvoeiro (tel. 2 82 35 65 94 | www.divers-cove.com)* offers diving courses and excursions all year round, including wreck diving.

The company *Portitours (tel. 2 82 47 00 13 | www.portitours.pt)* offers jeep tours and more.

ENTERTAINMENT

In the bars and clubs of the suburb *Praia da Rocha* is where it's all happening. At night in the summer, there is a lot going on along the main street.

TEATRO MUNICIPAL DE PORTIMÃO
TEMPO located in the former city palace Sárrea is host to all kinds of cultural events. Live music performed in its *Café Concerto. Ticket booth Tue–Sat 1:30–6:30pm, when events are on open until 9:30pm | Largo 1° Dezembro | tel. 2 82 40 24 75 | www.teatromunicipalde portimao.pt*

ALGARVE WINE

Many vineyards in the Algarve have been awarded various medals for their vintage wines, the quality of which is thanks to Portugal's ocean climate and excellent soil. White wines are characterised by their citrus colours and subtle, fruity flavours while their rosé wines offer hints of raspberry and the full-bodied red wines are full of character. Wine-tasting is offered by some of these vineyards where you can also buy bottles directly from the producer such as at the Adega *Quinta do Morgado da Torre (Sítio da Penina | direction is signposted off the N 125 | tel. 2 82 47 68 66 | www.morgadodatorre.com).* If you book in advance, you can also take a guided tour of vineyards such as the *Quinta do Francês (tel. 2 82 10 63 03 | www.quintadofrances.com)* in Odelouca near Silves. The luxury vineyard *Quinta dos Vales (Sítio dos Vales | Estômbar | tel. 2 82 43 10 36 | www.quintadosvales.eu)* near Carvoeiro also offers accommodation in one of its farmhouses *(Expensive).*

Amazing view – between Alvor and Portimão is Praia dos Três Irmãos beach

WHERE TO STAY

ALVOR PRAIA

A five-star complex with all the comforts – situated in a park at the stunning *Praia dos Três Irmãos* – that has you wanting for nothing. *195 rooms | tel. 2 82 40 09 00 | www.pestana.com | Expensive*

CASA DO RIO ARADE

A rustic manor house from the 18th century with nine pretty, light guest rooms and a pool. *Rua D. João II 33 | Mexilhoeira da Carregação | tel. 2 82 42 32 02 | www.rio arade.com | Moderate*

CASA TRÊS PALMEIRAS

Located on the cliffs at the end of the Praia do Vau this former private villa offers its guests an exclusive atmosphere as well as rest and relaxation on the spacious terrace by the pool. *5 rooms | tel. 2 82 40 12 75 | www.casatrespalmeiras. com | Expensive*

INFORMATION

POSTO DE TURISMO

Largo 1° Dezembro | tel. 2 82 40 24 87 | www.visitportimao.pt

WHERE TO GO

ALCALAR – MONUMENTOS MEGALÍTICOS (136 A4) (*F5*)

In Alvor's hinterland you'll find the small megalithic complex of Alcalar. Head in the direction of Lagos on the N 125, turn to the right (signposted) and after 4.6 km/2.9 miles you will reach the archaeological site. The impressive megalithic graves bear testimony to the leaders of a prehistoric culture dating back to the Stone Age. The structures have withstood both the ravages of time and efforts to plunder them. The restored complex invites you to take a walk back in time through a history dating back 5,000 years. Do not expect grand buildings he

posted INSIDER TIP *Zona Ribeirinha* with its wide promenade and pleasant restaurants and bars including the basic and inexpensive *Taberna Zé Morgadinho (Budget)*; above the harbour towers the overbearing and clumsily built parish church *Igreja Matriz*.

Alvor's sandy beach is also rewarding. Follow the INSIDER TIP flat paths behind the dunes, partly over wooden walkways, to the other side of the *Ria de Alvor*. These small walks offer excellent opportunities for a spot of bird-watching!

AUTÓDROMO INTERNACIONAL ALGARVE
(135 F3) (*ɯ E6*)

Architect Ricardo Pina designed the 4.692 m/2.915 miles racing circuit with its modern facilities, among them a go-cart track, an offroad park and apartments. The project cost more than 200 million euro and was controversial from the start. The Le-Mans Series has been held here as well as motorbike races. The course leads through undisturbed nature almost in its entire length. *In Mexilhoeira Grande | www.autodromoalgarve.com*

though. The booth at the entrance provides additional information. *Tue–Sat 10am–1pm and 2–6pm, in the winter 10am–1pm and 2–4:30pm | admission 2 euros (reduced joint ticket with Portimão Museum 4 euros).*

ALVOR (136 A5) (*ɯ F6*)

The *Ria de Alvor* is a wonderfully quiet tidal lagoon in an environmentally protected area and is the heart and soul of the surrounding area. Although a number of hotel complexes have sprung up at the edge of the fishing village of Alvor west of Portimão, on the eastern side of the river, but it has retained an appealing atmosphere which is best experienced on a stroll through the village.

In the modest centre in the upper part of the village, you'll find a small market and the humble remains of the Caste-lo de Alvor, a medieval fortress dating back to the 12th century. A more appealing alternative is the harbour area sign-

CARVOEIRO
(136 C6) (*ɯ G7*)

As recently as in the late 20th century, fishermen set the tone at "charburners' beach", but for a long time now, tourism prevails. Today the holiday town (population of 2,800) oscillates between groundedness and an aura of exclusivity because the area especially towards the east, as far as *Praia de Benagil,* is full of villas and luxury holiday resorts. *Carvoeiro-Clube (tel. 2 82 35 08 00 | www.carvoeirovillas.com | Moderate–Expensive)* coordinates several resorts with luxury villas, apartments and golf courses.

PORTIMÃO

The upper part of Carvoeiro offers more basic accommodation at *Casa Luiz (4 apartments | Rampa Nossa Senhora da Encarnação 5 | tel. 2 82 35 40 58 | www. casaluiz.com | Budget–Moderate)*. This bustling town offers rows on rows of restaurants, a popular meeting point is the *Grand Café (Largo da Praia | tel. 2 82 35 05 90 | Budget)*.

One thing you absolutely have to treat yourself to is an excursion from the Carvoeiro town centre to *Algar Seco*, preferably on foot. It is just 1,000 m/0.6 mile away. Along this stretch of coast the rocks have been worn down by the elements into particularly impressive and bizarre formations. A splendid **INSIDER TIP** wooden boardwalk path takes you over the heights of Carvoeiro which starts at the modern church (hardly recognisable as a church) situated in the town's upper part. This spectacular sight-seeing path takes you above the cliffs and ends at a car park with stairs leading down to the small *Boneca Bar* restaurant only open during the season *(tel. 2 82 35 83 91 | Budget – Moderate)*. Behind it, a short tunnel leads to a ⚜ double archway in the rock. The view of the cliffs rising perpendicularly all the way around the bay is captivating!

FERRAGUDO ⭐ (136 B5) (*M F6*)

If you look upward in Ferragudo (population of 1,900) and see houses clinging precariously to the slope, while in front of you lies the harbour full of colourful boats, you'll be pleasantly surprised. This fishing town lies 4 km/2.5 miles to the east of Portimão. It revolves around a pleasant central square with its selection of restaurants. Close to the square, a branch of the art gallery *Arte Algarve (Rua 25 de Abril 55–57)* opens its doors. The real gem of this picturesque town is revealed when you walk or drive along the Rio Arade to the *Praia Grande* by foot or by car and you will see the 14th century harbour fort *São João do Arade* looming large. From its perch on a slight rise it guards the mouth of the Rio. The Italian-looking complex is guarded by high walls and cannot be visited. Above the river mouth, cleverly blending in with nature, is the *Hotel ⚜ Casabela (63 rooms | Vale de Areia | tel. 2 82 49 06 50 | www.hotel-casabela.com | Expensive)* with magnificent views of the sea.

Ferragudo has a number of bars, atmospheric live music pubs and restaurants. One thing is certain, they all think that it is very important to have the sort of friendly atmosphere that is reminiscent of a small village. At the quay, fish restau-

One of the most picturesque resorts of the Algarve: Ferragudo

rants beckon; some have their barbecues going on the quay wall.

LAGOA
(136 C5) (*M G6*)

If you were to bypass this small town located 11 km/7 miles east of Portimão (population of 6,100) on the congested N 125, you would be missing out on a beautiful spot. Its historic core is pure 18th century, its heart is the small market hall and it is also home to some good restaurants.

The *Adega do Algarve* is an old wine production site. It is housed in a large complex directly on the N 125 in the middle of Lagoa. Visits and wine tastings are possible, and you can buy wines at low prices. In the same building complex, the *Edifício Adega de Lagoa,* has opened the doors of its INSIDERTIP *Galeria Arte Algarve (March–Nov Mon–Sat 10am–6pm | www.artealgarve.net)*, southern Portugal's largest gallery. This is a very ambitious private project financed without any public funding and used by many artists to display their works. The annual highlight is its summer exhibition where a moderate admission fee is charged to finance the extra concerts and other events organised.

PRAIA DA ROCHA (136 B5) (*M F6*)

This suburb (population of 3,600), 2 km/1.25 miles south of Portimão, is internationally well known and more famous than Portimão itself. In the 17th century a fort, the INSIDERTIP *Fortaleza de Santa Catarina*, was built above the mouth of the Rio Arade to protect the harbour from attacks. The fort was rebuilt after the earthquake in 1755 and now offers an excellent view of the ocean, the new yacht harbour, the Rio, Ferragudo and the surrounding area. There is not much left of the fort, but admission is free, and from up there, you can take the stairs down to the pier and the beach. Praia da Rocha was where tourism in the Algarve had its beginnings at the start of the 20th century when it was a favourite with the wealthy who built themselves their art nouveau villas. Today Praia da Rocha (along with Albufeira and Armação der Pêra) is the hotel hub of Barlavento. This is thanks to its beautiful namesake beach. A casino, bars and clubs make for a vibrant nightlife during high season, almost comparable with that of Albufeira. *Posto de Turismo (Av. Tomás Cabreira | tel. 2 82 41 91 32).*

If you take the coastal road to Alvor you will come across the beach bar INSIDERTIP *Caniço (April–Sept | at the Prainha holiday resort on the Praia do Vau-Praia dos Tres Irmãos Street | tel. 2 82 45 85 03 | Moderate)*, built within the cliffs and you get there by taking a lift down to sea level.

SAGRES

(134 A–B6) (*M B8*) Portugal's pride in its heritage is reflected in the name of the town. For ★ Sagres is synonymous with Infante Dom Henrique (Prince Henry the Navigator), the forefather of its marine discoveries.

It was the Prince's vision to turn his country, squeezed between Spain on the one side and the Atlantic on the other, into a seafaring nation. He succeeded in doing so with the help of marine navigation and a new type of ship, the caravel. Within two generations insignificant Portugal had turned into Europe's wealthiest country.

It has to be said though that very little of this history can be discerned here today, only perhaps at the *Fortaleza*. Lying just 1,000 m/0.6 mile outside the town, this castle complex dating back to the 17th century cordons off the *Ponta de Sagres*, a barren rock plateau that forms the point of this cape and stretches into the rolling ocean. All around are rugged cliff faces with a 60 m/200 ft or so sheer drop. The *Ponta* represents the counterpart to *São Vicente* or Cape St Vincent, as well as the starting point of the Barlavento coast. From ⚜ the western cliff edge there is an unforgettable view of the bay of Beliche and São Vicente, while the eastern cliff edge gives you a view of Sagres

with the offshore Martinhal islands and the ● *fishing harbour.*

As you take in this spectacular sight you can imagine just how the Prince and his men once stood here more than 500 years ago and dreamed of the far off lands they would discover. Granted that Henry (based in nearby Lagos) may have been the "manager" of the maritime expeditions that made history, it was here, "at the end of the old world", between the capes of Sagres and São Vicente that the "brainstorming" would have taken place. If it is a romantic destination you are after then Sagres is the place, as it is for sun worshippers who prefer to spend the day at the beach! Irrespective of which way the wind blows, Sagres always has sheltered and protected beaches. The tides change daily, occasionally the Gulf Stream current reaches the bays ... and at times not. This ocean current makes for constantly changing weather conditions. Surfers, divers and fishermen alike, rate Europe's most south-westerly spot as the continent's number one.

THE ALGARVE ON A BIKE

Ecovia (www.ecoviasalgarve.org) is a 214 km/133 miles long cycle route along the Algarve offering cyclists the chance to discover the stretch between Cabo de São Vicente in the west and the Rio Guadiana in the east bordering on Spain. The route is signposted with small yellow poles at the sides and blue lines on the road. Information boards are also provided yet directions are not always immediately clear. The Ecovia mostly runs along the coastline next to the sea albeit for a stretch taking you inland around the resort complex.

Although the route becomes a challenge in the cities of Tavira, Faro, Portimão and Lagos, it then continues past golf courses, almond and fig trees and then takes you back to the coast. Bikers share approximately 12 percent of the route with cars and some stretches are also suitable for hikers. Birdwatching is also an option along the entire route particularly at the Ria Formosa but also around Sagres, a popular stopover for birds migrating south. Bikes can be hired from *Megasport (www.megasport.pt)*.

Rosa dos ventos – the "wind rose" or compass in Sagres' Fortaleza

The Fortaleza may be one of the most visited attractions of the Algarve but the small town (pop. 2,000) benefits very little from all the tourist traffic. It has a casual, pleasant atmosphere but without a real town centre it lacks the charm of a town. On fishing days, the big fish auction takes place at the harbour at 10am.

Also attributed to Prince Henry is the wind rose or wind compass marked out with pieces of stone which was rediscovered in 1928. There is still some debate among scientists who believe it may not have been a compass because it has 42 marks as opposed to the usual 36. The age of the 43 m/1,41 ft in diameter wind rose is just as uncertain.

SIGHTSEEING

FORTALEZA

You enter the imposing castle wall through a winding entrance dating back to the 17th century. Unfortunately the modern museum behind it – with strong contrasts between the old and the new – is a travesty. *(May, June, Sept Tue–Sun 9:30am–8:30pm | Oct–April 9:30am–5:30pm | admission 3 euros).* An enchanting chapel is located alongside the new complex and you would be forgiven for thinking that its bell tower is a miniature version of the unpretentious and harmonious architecture that characterises the Algarve. This is supposedly what is left of Prince Henry's "School of Navigation" that was once based here.

FOOD & DRINK

ESTRELA DO MAR

A popular meeting spot for locals as well as tourists serving fish specialties, wines and beer. *Rua Comandante Matoso | tel. 2 82 62 40 65 | Budget*

NORTADA

Windsurfers are not the only ones to frequent this popular restaurant on Martinhal beach. Fresh fish is always served; the fish dish will depend on what the local fishermen have caught on the day. *Mobile tel. 9 18 61 34 10 | Moderate*

VILA VELHA

This top quality restaurant is elegant and relaxed. The quality of its cuisine has made it a top address in Sagres. Excellent wines to accompany the dishes. *Rua António Patrão Faustino | tel. 2 82 62 47 88 | www.vilavelha-sagres.com | Moderate–Expensive*

BEACHES

The *Praia da Mareta* is close to the town and is sheltered from the west wind. Immediately behind Sagres is the *Praia do Tonel* which is more exposed to the wind and which also gets some high waves. The *Praia do Martinhal* is a haven for windsurfers. It lies behind the fishing harbour and has a picturesque setting of offshore islands – bird paradise! The *Praia do Beliche* is a favourite with surfers due to its fabulous waves. It lies 3 km/1.8 miles on the road leading to Cabo de São Vicente.

SPORTS & ACTIVITIES

Sagres is a surfers' stronghold. Once a bastion for windsurfers, it has now also been discovered by the surfing fraternity. A number of surfing schools come here to conduct courses in the district. The resident surf school is *Freeride Surf School (mobile tel. 9 18 75 54 01 | freeridesurf camp.com)*.

The waters surrounding Sagres are among the richest in Europe in terms of abundance of fish and wealth of species. No wonder then that it is a popular place for recreational fishing. At Sagres harbour you can also book boat trips along the coast as well as dolphin watching trips (July–Sept). There you will also find the diving school *Divers Cape (tel. 2 82 62 43 70 | www.diverscape.com)*.

Bird watching is also very popular around Sagres. Starting at the beginning of the main migration period in October, the four-day ✪ *Festival de Birdwatching de Sagres* takes place *(www.birdwatchingsagres.com)*.

WHERE TO STAY

MARTINHAL BEACH RESORT & HOTEL

An extensive, exclusive family-friendly hotel complex on the hilltop over the beach in Martinhal. Besides the hotel, the village also has rows of houses and villas. If you decide not to overnight here, try instead the excellent cuisine at one of the village's three restaurants, the *O Terraço (Expensive)*. *37 rooms | 99 houses and villas | Praia do Martinhal | tel. 2 82 24 02 00 | www.martinhal.com | Expensive*

MEMMO BALEEIRA ⚶

Its idyllic location above the fishing harbour of Sagres scores it plenty of points. A contemporary, white designer hotel, with a relaxed surfer-chic atmosphere, offering it predominantly young international clientele a great bar, beautiful rooms and unrivalled views. *144 rooms and suites | Sitio da Baleeira | tel. 2 82 62 42 12 | www.memmohotels.com | Moderate*

PONTALAIA

22 sophisticated apartments tastefully decorated, some with a sea view. Pool and sauna. Very affordable in off-peak seasons. *Rua Infante D. Henrique | tel. 2 82 62 02 80 | www.pontalaia.com | Moderate*

INFORMATION

POSTO DE TURISMO

Av. Comandante Matoso | tel. 2 82 62 48 73 | www.cm-viladobispo.pt

Waiting to ride the next wave – surfers at the Praia do Tonel

WHERE TO GO

CABO DE SÃO VICENTE
(134 A6) (*ɯ B7*)

If you are visiting Sagres, a visit to *Cape St Vincent,* Europe's most south-westerly point, is a must (see p. 89). It is a 5 km/3 miles drive and its landmark lighthouse beacon is visible for 90 km/56 miles, standing bold and tall amid a spectacular natural setting of wind and waves.

NOSSA SENHORA DE GUADALUPE
(134 C5) (*ɯ C7*)

On the road to Lagos, just before you get to Raposeira 15 km/9 miles from Sagres is an isolated chapel dating back to the 14th century, its beauty and simplicity never fails to impress. *Closed Mon*

PRAIAS DA FIGUEIRA/DO ZAVIAL/DA INGRINA(134 B–C 5–6) (*ɯ C7*)

You can get to these three heavenly beaches by car from *Raposeira* (between Sagres and Vila do Bispo). They are about 18 km/11 miles away from Sagres between some magnificent rocky coves. The **INSIDER TIP** *Praia do Zavial* is a real gem of a beach, even though at high tide it is almost completely submerged.

VILA DO BISPO
(134 B5) (*ɯ B–C7*)

This inland resort (1,000 inhabitants) lies 8 km/5 miles to the north of Sagres and its landmark is the old *water tower* perched at the town's highest point. The church on the town's square is worth a look inside as well as the indoor market hall located just outside the main hub; if you have time, take the **INSIDER TIP** hiking trail that leads past the market hall all the way to the Cabo de São Vicente, 13 km/8 miles away from Vila do Bispo and along the clifftops – a spectacular trail!

THE SOTAVENTO

The sandy Algarve begins at Vilamoura with the Quinta do Lago/Praia do Ancão and goes all the way to the mouth of the Rio Guadiana on the Spanish border. A large part of this area is the 60 km/37 miles long nature reserve Ria Formosa.

The coast is flat with dunes that are often lined with pine forests. The atmosphere here is different to that of the rocky Algarve: the tranquillity of the hinterland spills over all the way to the coast.

FARO

🟦 **MAP INSIDE BACK COVER**
(139 E5–6) (*M7–8*) Many tourists only use the Algarve capital for its airport – this means visitors may inad- vertently miss out on its attractive historic centre.

Faro's old city, *Vila-Adentro* (also: Cidade Velha), is a walled time capsule in the middle of a busy city (population of 60,000). Entering it at the access points in the well-preserved city wall (dating back to both Romans and Moors), you may believe that you have stepped into another world.

In 713 the Moors conquered the harbour (previously under Phoenician and Roman control) and called it "harúm". They developed it into a trading port and safeguarded it with a fort. In 1249 Christian Crusaders captured the fort. The conquest is displayed on *azulejos* on the *Arco do Repouso* city gate. In 1755 the entire city was destroyed by the massive earth

Where beach and sea seem to go on forever: a sun-kissed coast, wide sandy beaches, salines and pretty towns await you

quake. Very few architectural elements remained intact. The *Sé Catedral* was one that could be restored. The remaining buildings inside the city wall date back to the 18th century. Outside the walls, a network of alleyways spreads into the busy city centre with its pedestrian zone. The views over the harbour and the lagoon of Ria Formosa are also spectacular. White storks bring a touch of nature to the city. Faro's tourist image has recently undergone change. Thanks to frequent flights from Germany and the UK, many young-er people now take long-weekend breaks here to soak up the sun on the nearby beaches and hit the student city's night-life. Hostels are popping up everywhere to meet this increase in demand.

SIGHTSEEING

CENTRO CIÊNCIA VIVA DO ALGARVE ●

A former power station on the banks of the Ria directly outside the city walls with interactive exhibits where the ongoing environmental damage to the sea can be viewed. A hit on a rainy day especially with children and teenagers who will also have fun learning from the exhibits. A nice attraction is the INSIDER TIP ▶ "touch and feel" pool with starfish, sea cucumbers, hermit crabs and small sea urchins. *Tue–Sun 10am–6pm | admission 4 euros | Rua Comandante Francisco Manuel | www.ccvalg.pt*

Bizarre bone art – *Capela dos Ossos* in the Igreja do Carmo

CONVENTO NOSSA SENHORA DA ASSUNÇÃO ●

Magnificent Renaissance architecture with a two-storey cloister and a pretty garden. The only contact that the Poor Clare nuns who lived here in the past had with the outside world was to peep through the wooden slits in the tower on the roof of the complex. The Convento also houses the *Museu Municipal* (see below), which is well worth a visit. *Largo Alfonso III 14*

IGREJA NOSSA SENHORA DO CARMO

The ossuary chapel *(Capela dos Ossos)* in this baroque church on the *Largo do Carmo* square (about 1,000 m/0.6 mile from the Vila-Adentro) displays this rather ominous warning above its entrance: "Take heed for you too will end up like this one day". The chapel's ceiling and walls are "embellished" with skulls, but strangely enough this does not come across as morbid as one would expect it to. *Mon–Fri 10am–1pm and 2pm–5pm (in the summer until 6pm), Sat 10am–1pm | admission 2 euros*

IGREJA DE SÃO FRANCISCO

Valuable *azulejo* pictures and gilded wood carvings decorate this single-nave church dating back to the 16th century, situated some 200m from the Arco de Repouso city gate. In the former *abbey garden* behind the Cidade Velha you will see surface reliefs with mystical representations on the hexagonal granary *(celeiro)*.

MUSEU MUNICIPAL

It houses fascinating artefacts from the times of the Romans, Visigoths and Moors, as well as jewellery, old weapons and coins and a picture gallery well worth seeing. *June–Sept Tue–Fri 10am–7pm, Sat/Sun 11:30am–6pm, Oct–May Tue–Fri 10am–6pm, Sat/Sun 10:30am–5pm | admission 2 euros | Largo Alfonso III 14 | inside the Convento behind the Sé*

SÉ ☼☼

Faro Cathedral locally known as Sé looms large in the old city. It has a very interesting mix of styles. The architecture dating back to 1251 was built on top of the ruins of a mosque. The mighty Gothic bell tower dates back to this period and there is an excellent view of the area from the top. Admire the *azulejos* and the ornate baroque organ in the Chapel of the Rosary. The organ is a masterpiece of its time *(Mon–Fri 10am–6pm (in the winter until 5pm, Sat 10am–1pm | admission 3 euros).* Opposite the Sé and on the southerly side of the Largo Dom Afonso III square is the palatial *Paço Episcopal*, which remains the seat of the bishop to this day.

VILA-ADENTRO (OLD TOWN) ★

It only has a diameter of some 500 m/1,640 ft and is completely surrounded by a medieval wall. There are imposing architecture examples from different centuries but the real charm of the old city lies in the cobblestone alleyways, the small shops, restaurants and cosy nooks all beckoning you to take a stroll and explore.

FOOD & DRINK

O CASTELO ● ☼☼

This restaurant's main attraction is maybe not its cuisine (although it does serve a good, home-style salmon at an affordable price) but its unique setting next to the city walls and a top spot to watch the sunset occasionally accompanied by live music. A great atmosphere to be enjoyed among the city's locals. *Near Largo do Castelo | mobile tel. 9 19 84 64 05 | Budget–Moderate*

FAZ GOSTOS

Situated within the city walls, this is an exclusive address for fine dining. It specialises in modern interpretations of classic Portuguese cuisine at relatively affordable prices with a selection of different menus available. *Rua do Castelo 13 | tel. 2 89 87 84 22 | Expensive*

VIVMAR

The local association of fishers supplies this restaurant with the freshest fish. And you can taste the difference – its seafood and shellfish are delicious. *Closed Sun | Rua Comandante Francisco Manuel 8 | mobile tel. 9 16 14 55 84 | Budget–Moderate*

SHOPPING

The shopping centre ● *Forum Algarve (www.forumalgarve.net)* is located out-

---

★ **Vila-Adentro (Old town)**
Faro's historical old city –
a medieval island amid the
modern world → **p. 59**

★ **Milreu**
Roman traces with beautiful
mosaics → **p. 61**

★ **Tavira**
Picturesque: a river, churches, a
small castle and an historical
bridge → **p. 63**

★ **Igreja de São Lourenço**
Baroque chapel beautifully
embellished with *azulejo* walls
→ **p. 69**

★ **Armona & Culatra**
Hop on to a ferry and explore
the offshore islands → **p. 60**

★ **Alcoutim**
Sleepy fortress town on the
Rio Guadiana → **p. 72**

MARCO POLO HIGHLIGHTS

side the city centre with a wide selection of shops selling items from fashion jewellery to sporting gear. It also has a cinema and the usual fast-food restaurants.

BEACH

PRAIA DE FARO

Faro's own beach on the Ilha de Faro is 10 km/6 miles long! In the Seventies a building spree took place here and house after house sprung up on the dunes, all jammed as close as possible. The locals who spend the entire summer or weekends here have plenty of restaurants to choose from. The wave-free lagoon behind the dune is a hit for windsurfers who do rapid sprints here; the kitesurfers are even faster. *Access via the road at the airport*

SPORTS & ACTIVITIES

Lands (Edifício Ginásio Clube Naval | Doca de Recreiode | Faro | tel. 2 89 8174 66 | www.lands.pt) ventures out to sea from Faro's harbour in small INSIDER TIP sailing boats or kayaks to explore the *Ria Formosa*.

ENTERTAINMENT

Bars, clubs and pubs – for a thriving nightlife, head for the area behind the Avenida da República, especially in the Travessa José Coelho and the Rua do Prior. This nightlife centre is home to pubs, bars etc. and goes by the curious name of *Rua do Crime,* or "Street of crimes". It is the destination for many students studying in Faro. Head to *Maktub (Rua do Compromisso)* and *Ditadura (Largo da Madalena)* for live music and the *First Floor Club (Rua do Prior)* if you're looking to dance the night away.

The *Teatro das Figuras (Horta das Figuras | www.teatrodasfiguras.pt)* and *Teatro Lethes (Rua de Portugal 58 | www.actateatro.org.pt/teatrolethes)* both offer exciting cultural programs.

WHERE TO STAY

DOM BERNARDO

Pleasant, comfortable hotel in the *Rua General Teófilo da Trindade 20. 43 rooms | tel. 2 89 88 98 00 | www.bestwestern.es/hotel-dombernardo | Moderate*

FARO

Modern four-star city hotel slightly lacking in character yet with restaurant (roof terrace) and beach club. *90 rooms | Praça D. Francisco Gomes 2 | tel. 2 89 83 08 30 | www.hotelfaro.pt | Moderate*

INFORMATION

POSTO DE TURISMO

Rua da Misericórdia 8–11 | tel. 2 89 80 36 04 | www.cm-faro.pt

WHERE TO GO

ARMONA & CULATRA ★

A ferry will take you across to this dune islands from the Cais Comercial and the Cais das Portas do Mar. The ride it alone is well worth it for the spectacular views of the coastline and Ria Formosa. Life on the islands is a world in itself (without any cars) – very Portuguese and very neighbourly.

The fishing harbour on *Culatra (139 F6–140 A6) (ṁ N8)* – also the name of the main resort – is one of the most picturesque settings throughout the south of Portugal. Set slightly back from the harbour is the excellent restaurant ● ﾐ *Janoca (tel. 2 89 05 01 53 | Moderate)* serving delicious fish and with splendid views over the Algarve landscape. An other destination on the island is *Far* with its lighthouse that can be seen from far; a lot of privately owned houses are rented out here in summer. In contrast, the resort is deserted in winter. Some of the small houses on *Armona* (140 A–B5)

ESTÓI & MILREU (139 F4) (*M N7*)

The relaxed town of Estói (population of 3,500) lies 9 km/6 miles northeast of Faro. It is home to a magnificent architectural feat, the rococo-style palace of the

Some of the splendid Roman floor mosaics in Milreu have been well-preserved

(*M O7–8*) can also be rented. The island has a camping site and some restaurants and cafés which are open in summer.

CABO DE SANTA MARIA
(139 E6) (*M M8*)

Portugal's most southerly point on the *Ilha Deserta* about 8 km/5 miles from Faro is uninhabited, however in the summer it makes for a popular excursion for beach goers, mussel, clam and cockle collectors and fishermen. Ships sail from Faro during the main season. The gourmet restaurant ☙ *Estaminé (tel. 17 81 18 56 | ilha-deserta.com | ⸱ensive)* (reserve!) is also a real architectural treasure. Its snack bar offers a affordable alternative.

Visconde de Estói *Palácio de Estói,* which is encased in a repellent modern cover. Inside is now a hotel, the *Pousada (63 rooms | tel. 2 10 40 76 20 | www.pousadas.pt | Moderate–Expensive).* Parts of the small, beautiful park are also accessible to non-guests, as are the old salons of the Pousada (access is past reception).

The ★ Milreu Roman ruins (139 E4) (*M M7*) *(May–Sept Tue–Sun 9:30am–1pm and 2pm–6:30pm, Oct–April Tue–Sun 9am–1pm and 2pm–5:30pm | admission 2 euros)* are near Estói, approximately 600 m/1,970 ft from the town centre on the road to Faro. The ruins are the remains of a villa. Well preserved mosaics in the baths depict leaping dolphins. A small temple from the 4th century was turned into an early Christian sanctuary by the Visigoths in the 6th century.

OLHÃO (139–140 F5–A5) *(ꖴ N7)*

The town (population 15,000) some 8 km/5 miles east of Faro, is characterised by its enormous harbour with its bustling traffic of boats. The promenade is neatly kept and the road opposite (Av. 5 de

promenade; one of them houses the fishmongers. You won't find a larger fish market anywhere else on the Algarve – there's a massive variety of fish.

There is no doubt about it, Olhão is at its best on a Saturday when the square between the shore and the market halls plays host to an additional fruit and vegetable market. From the harbour, there's a boat service to the islands of Armona and Culatra. *www.cm-olhao.pt*

Tavira: The seven-arch Ponte Romana dating back to the 17th century crosses the Rio Gilão

Outubro) is lined with fish restaurants; the *O Bote (Av. 5 de Outoubro | tel. 2 89 72 11 83 | Moderate)* has a good reputation for its barbecued fish. It's worth taking a stroll along its small streets to the *Igreja Matriz*. In the rear of the main church, the outer *Capela do Senhor dos Aflitos*, candles burn day and night, a place for family members to pray for the safe return of their fishermen. Next to it is the colourful hive of activity around the two restored market halls on the

SÃO BRÁS DE ALPORTEL (139 F3) *(ꖴ N6)*

A placid provincial town located some 15 km/9 miles north with an interesting museum of local history, the ● *Museu do Traje* in the town centre *(Mon–Fri 10am– 1pm and 2–5pm, Sat/Sun 2–5pm | admission 2 euros | Rua Dr. José Dias Sancho 61 | www.museu-sbras.com)*. The museum displays an interesting collection of traditional costumes and dress while informative permanent exhibition side the main building concentrates on cork production. The spacious courtyard at the back (with historical carriages under the shelter) also houses the *Cantinho do Museu (Budget)* bar, ideal if you're in search of food and refreshment. The museum also offers a diverse **INSIDER TIP** cultural program usually with jazz performances on the third Sunday in the month, fado on the last Sunday in the month and other concerts in between.

TAVIRA

MAP INSIDE BACK COVER
(140 C3–4) (*m* P6) The Rio Gilão divides the former Phoenician harbour city ⭐ Tavira in two halves, picturesquely linked by the so-called Roman bridge (Ponte Romano). Tavira is also a city of churches, with more than 20 built over time.

Patrician houses line the river bank, testimony to a time of economic prosperity from the once-thriving tuna, wine and salt trade. The city became so important in the 16th century that the king officially declared it a metropolis of the Kingdom of the Algarve. However by the 19th century its demise had begun to set in. In more recent decades however, tourism has succeeded in giving the town (population of 12,500) a new-found splendour.

It is worth taking your time when you explore Tavira, on each side of the river. Only then will you experience its peaceful charm and begin to understand why so many visitors as well as its residents, consider this the Algarve's most charming city. Browse the *Travessa de D. Brites*, which is Tavira's showcase, then walk along the *Rua D. Marcelino Franco* to end up at *Nossa Senhora das Ondas* (church of "Our lady of the Waves") dating back

to the 17th century. *Praça da República* with its cafés and restaurants is Tavira's focal point; the square is situated on the riverfront at the imposing Roman bridge. Also off the square is the *Jardim Público* offering visitors some welcome shade with its lush palms and plants. At the park's centre stands an old music pavilion, from where the coastal promenade goes on to the former market hall, a beautiful old iron structure. Restaurant after restaurant can be found here, in the perfect setting – right by the river.

SIGHTSEEING

CAMERA OBSCURA / TORRE DE TAVIRA

Housed in the old water tower, the camera obscura projects live images of Tavira onto a large screen with its lens system – an interesting and exciting attraction geared towards families with children. Through the optical lens of the camera obscura – you have a view right across to the salt marshes. *Mon–Fri 10am–4/5pm, Sat 10am–1pm | admission 4 euros | Calçada da Galeria 12*

LOW BUDGET

Behind the lagoon beach in Fuseta is the *Parque Campismo (tel. 2 89 79 34 59 | camping@uf-moncarapacho-fuseta.pt)* offering extremely affordable prices for tents, mobile homes and caravans.

● Tootle from Olhão to the *Ilhas Armona* or *Culatra* by ferry (return ticket 5–6,50 euros), collect *ameijoas* (cockles), then prepare them for dinner yourself.

CASTELO ● ☼

Only a few parts of the fortress and the Roman-Moorish city wall have survived. To reach it, go up *Rua Galeria* next to the Praça da República square. Enjoy a view of Tavira's unique roofscape from the *garden* of the fortress. Admission is free. *Mon–Fri 8am–5pm, Sat/Sun 9am–5pm*

IGREJA DA MISERICÓRDIA

This imposing building is located at the entrance to the fort. The Renaissance church built in 1541 is by the same architect André Pilarte whose talent was first seen in Lisbon's world-famous Jerónimos Monastery. Architecture enthusiasts regard *Igreja da Misericórdia's* Renaissance portal, its gilded altar and *azulejos* among the country's most beautiful.

IGREJA DE SANTA MARIA

This harmoniously structured three-nave building towers up close to the fort walls. In the 13th century, a Gothic church that also served as a place of refuge was built on top of the Moorish ruin (of which the portal and two side chapels have been retained) before undergoing a Manueline refurbishment later on. After the earthquake of 1755 the famous Italian architect Francisco Fabri was given the task to reconstruct it. A second entrance leads to a side wing of the building with an *exhibition on sacred art (closed Sat afternoons and Sun)*

IGREJA DE SÃO JOSÉ

An unusually shaped church to the south of the town centre: its sides have unequal lengths. Also features a Gothic and a Manueline side chapel and a high altar with trompe-l'oeil paintings. *Praça Zacarias Guerreiro*

PALÁCIO DA GALERIA

This representative building houses changing art exhibitions; at the entrance, excavation remains from the 7th/6th century BC can be seen under glass plates. Archaeological and ecclesiastical pieces

RIA FORMOSA

A 60 km/37 miles chain of dunes separates the *Ria Formosa* from the Atlantic. The expansive lagoon formed as a result of the undersea earthquake in 1755 stretches along the Sotavento coastline from Quinta do Lago in the west to the Praia da Manta Rota in the east. It is a constantly changing landscape with the calm mudflats at high tide gradually turning into a network of water channels when the tide is low. Aside from the swarms of migratory birds that turn up here for the winter, some very rare bird and animal species are also found here e.g. fiddler crabs, chameleons and purple moorhens. There are numerous birds, plants, crustaceans, fish, reptiles, mussels, clams, cockles and shells and not least vast colonies of seahorses. Numerous *viveiros* (inconspicuous fish breeding facilities) produce around 10,000 tons of seafood annually. Organisers such as *Passeios Ria Formosa (mobile tel. 9 62 15 69 22 or 9 61 18 98 57 | www. passeios-ria-formosa.com)* offer guided tours by boat through the nature reserve, from starting points like Olhão, Fuseta, Cabanas de Tavira and Santa Luzia.

are show in a somewhat scattered manner. *Tue–Sat 10am–4:30pm | admission 2 euros*

FOOD & DRINK

A VER TAVIRA
Serves as a restaurant with fish and seafood on the menu as well as a piano bar with cocktails. Delightful terrace next to the castle's garden. *Calçada da Galeria 13 | tel. 2 81 38 13 63 | Moderate–Expensive*

BEIRA RIO
Pleasant restaurant in a peaceful setting directly on the Rio Gilão serving excellent international cuisine and good-quality wines from Portugal. *Rua Borda d'Água da Assêca | tel. 2 81 32 31 65 | Moderate*

PÁTIO
A gourmet restaurant in a nondescript street in one of the city's old mansions with a lovely terrace and great atmosphere. *Rua António Cabreira 30 | tel. 2 81 32 30 08 | Moderate*

ENTERTAINMENT

The old market hall on the river bank and the Praça da República – where street artists make for a great atmosphere even during the day – get very busy at night. There are some bars and restaurants with live music, e.g. *Álvaro de Campos (Rua da Liberdade 47)*. A top spot for the night life scene is *Mood (Dr. José Pires Padinha)*.

WHERE TO STAY

ALBACORA
Once the Algarve's greatest bastion of the tuna fishing industry, it is now home to a luxury hotel with an extra-large swimming pool and its own boat to the lagoon

Tavira – one of the Algarve's most beautiful towns

landscape of the Ria Formosa. *162 rooms | Quatro Águas | tel. 2 81 38 08 00 | www.vilagale.pt | Moderate–Expensive*

POUSADA CONVENTO DA GRAÇA
An upmarket hotel housed in a 16th century convent. Beautiful courtyard and park area with pool. *36 rooms | Rua Dom Paio Peres Correia | tel. 2 10 40 76 80 | www.pousadas.pt | Expensive*

QUINTA DOS POETAS

Isolated country hotel, nice rooms some with balcony, pool and a good restaurant. *22 rooms | between Moncarapacho and Santa Catarina | tel. 2 89 99 09 90 | www. quintadospoetas.com | Moderate*

INFORMATION

POSTO DE TURISMO
Praça da República 5 | tel. 2 81 32 25 11 | www.cm-tavira.pt

WHERE TO GO

CABANAS DE TAVIRA
(141 D3–4) (⌘ P6)

This may seem at first sight a rather un-impressive resort (2,000 inhabitants) 8 km/5 miles to the east of Tavira – however first impressions can be deceiving. It is in fact the boarding point for a ferry service sailing through the lagoon to the long stretch of beautiful beach at Praia de Cabanas. The resort also has a welcoming promenade providing benches to take a break as well as restaurants and accommodation including the self-catering option INSIDER TIP *Pedras da Rainha (140 studios/houses | on your right when you enter the village | tel. 2 81 38 06 80 | pedrasdarainha.com | Moderate).*

CACELA VELHA ☆ (141 D3) (⌘ Q6)

A small harbour fort dating back to the 12th century, a few dozen houses, the place has an idyllic setting above the Ria lagoon. Enjoy the views at the esplanade in front of the church which is also worth a visit. The INSIDER TIP *village cemetery* is also typical for the Algarve region with coffin drawers stacked one on top of the other.

INSIDER TIP FUSETA (140 B5) (⌘ O7)

This coastal resort (also written: Fuzeta; 2,000 inhabitants) lies 15 km/9 miles to

the south west and its attractive setting on the lagoon is particularly appealing to tourists – including a harbour, boat trips and lagoon beach. Among all the nice spots, one particular favourite is the bar *O Farol (Rua Professor César Oliveira | mobile tel. 9 36 06 43 69 | Budget)* with many seats on the terrace and occasional live music.

ILHA DE TAVIRA
(140 B–C 4–5) (⌘ O–P 6–7)

The 10 km/6 miles long dunes are a rare beauty. Boats set sail all year round from the *Quatro Águas* station just outside Tavira while in summer passengers usually board near Tavira's former indoor market hall. The Tavira island offers a row of restaurants and a camping site.

PRAIA DE CABANAS
(141 D3) (⌘ Q6)

A narrow strip of sand approximately 5 km/3 miles east of Tavira separates the Ria Formosa lagoon from the ocean. You can swim in the warm lagoon water on the one side, in the colder seawater on the other. Go foraging for mussels, clams, cockles and snails and cook up a feast with your bounty!

SANTA LUZIA (140 C4) (⌘ P7)

Santa Luzia, only 3 km/1.8 miles west of Tavira, is said to be a stronghold of octopus fishing. The harbour promenade offering views over the boats is appealing here while the resort also has a good restaurant, the INSIDER TIP *Vale d'el Rei (Expensive)* which belongs to the studio-apartment complex *Pedras d'el Rei (130 apartments | tel. 2 81 38 06 00 | www. pedrasdelrei.com | Moderate).*

A tourist train leaves close by taking passengers to the almost endless *Praia do Barril* or you can go by foot following the 1 km/0.6 mile path that runs next to the railway tracks. A curious attraction is the *anchor cemetery* behind the Barril beach where fishermen have "buried" around 200 of their rusty anchors. The *Barril Beach Café (Budget)* next to the train terminus is just one of the cafés to choose from.

VILAMOURA

(138 B–C4) (∅ K7) Vilamoura is a major hub showcasing the crème de la crème of holiday property. Man)y (often luxurious) vacation and golf complexes have sprung up within its 10 km/6 miles or so radius. Numerous yachts from all around the world visit the marina which has more than a thousand moorings. Dozens of restaurants, bars and shops line the waterfront and there is also a casino. That's why Vilamoura is the playground for Portugal's in-crowd from the fashion, film and football worlds. Who knows, you could even bump into a star when you visit one of the summer clubs on the marina, or while sipping a cocktail in football legend Luís Figo's *Bar 7*.

SIGHTSEEING

CERRO DA VILA

West of the yacht harbour you can visit a display of the findings from the excavation of a Roman villa and a fish factory. Processed sardines were exported from here to Rome as long as 2,000 years ago!

FOOD & DRINK

Although affordable authentic Portuguese restaurants may be hard to come by in Vilamoura, there is no shortage of pizzerias and restaurants serving Chinese, Indian and Mediterranean cuisine.

AKVAVIT

Serves exquisite seafood dishes and international specialities. *Edificio Vilamarina | tel. 2 89 38 07 12 | www.restauranteakvavit.com | Expensive*

Dining under palm trees: evening vibes in the marina at Vilamoura

EMO GOURMET

The fusion of traditional and innovative Portuguese cuisine combined with a min-imalistic-modern ambience works well in the Tivoli-Marina hotel. *Evenings only | Av. dos Descobrimentos | tel. 2 89 31 70 00 | www.tivolihotels.com | Expensive*

WILLIE'S

The German star chef Wilhelm Wurg-er has opted to serve excellent Mediter-ranean cuisine rather than typical Por-tuguese. Excellent food and wine menu. *Thu–Tue, evenings only | Rua do Brasil 2 | tel. 2 89 38 08 49 | www.willies-restau rante.com | Expensive*

BEACHES

Stretching to the west is *Praia da Rocha Baixinha* which merges into the chain of beaches of *Praia da Falésia*. To the east lie *Praias Vale do Lobo, Garrão, Ancão* and *Quinta do Lago*, the latter is accessed via a 320 m/1,050 ft wooden bridge.

SPORTS & ACTIVITIES

Board a boat trip setting off from the marina: you can choose between mo-tor boats and yachts for a whole day or sunset cruise. The "champagne cruise" is available for all connoisseurs.

ENTERTAINMENT

KADOC

Guests are shuttled to the high-tech disco *Kadoc* with the club's own buses. Parking spaces are available all around the capital building on the old road between Albufei-ra-Vilamoura. The club gets going around

BOOKS & FILMS

The Algarve Fish Book – A culinary guide to Southern Portugal by Nico Böer and Andrea Siebert which is full of fascinating facts and advice for foodies, chefs and seafood enthusiasts.

Journey to Portugal – A fascinating ac-count of Jose Saramago's voyage of dis-covery through his own country in his old motor car. He explores its history, religion, literature and culture in his own unique and entertaining manner.

Beyond the Sea – Stories from the Algarve – Lisa Salvidge sets her plot around a young English couple in search of an easier life in the sun. An interesting cast of characters whose lives intertwine against the rich tapestry of the Algarve.

The Immortals (Os Imortais) – A thriller about former members of a special commando in the colonial war of 1974 involved in shady undertakings and fick-le love affairs. It was made into a film Filmed by António Pedro Vasconcelos in 2003, partly set in Albufeira.

Fado Blues (Tudo isto é Fado) – This comedy is about two young Brazilian rogues who plan a spectacular burglary in Portugal. By Luís Galvão Teles, filmed in Lisbon in 2004.

A Luz na Ria Formosa – A documentary film by João Botelho (2005) whose cin-ematic skills serve to portray the Ria Formosa nature reserve in an especially atmospheric way.

The entire interior of the São Lourenço dos Matos chapel is adorned with azulejos

1 am and by 2 am the mood gets exuberant. *Sat from 11pm | admission around 20 euros | Cerca da Areia | www.kadoc.pt*

WHERE TO STAY

DOM PEDRO GOLF, MARINA AND PORTOBELO HOTELS

Three under one umbrella with more than 500 luxury rooms and suites, plus spa facilities. *Tel. 2 89 30 07 80 and 289 38 11 00 | www.dompedro.com | Expensive*

TIVOLI MARINA VILAMOURA

This massive five-star complex is set above the yacht harbour. Entertainment, restaurants, tennis and special golf programs. *380 rooms and suites | tel. 2 89 30 33 03 | www.tivolihotels.com | Expensive*

VILA GALÉ MARINA

Exemplary four-star complex on the marina. *243 rooms and suites | tel. 89 30 00 00 | www.vilagale.com | Moderate–Expensive*

WHERE TO GO

ALMANCIL (139 D4) (*Ø L7*)

The baroque church ★ ● *Igreja de São Lourenço (Mon 3–5pm, Tue–Sat 10am–1pm | admission 3 euros)* towers alongside the busy N 125 motorway. Its interior is entirely clad in blue and white *azulejos* telling the history of the martyr Lourenço. The hand carved gilded gallery is magnificent, as are the altar and choir stalls. Near the curch is the yoga centre ● *Quinta da Calma (tel. 2 89 39 37 41 | quinta-da-calma. com)*. The therapies on offer in the different wooden houses change constantly – a tiny village wi th a soulful calm.

Expensive shops, cafés and restaurants reside in Almancil thanks to the town's proximity to the stylish golf courses and holiday complexes. Even so, this town with a population of 4,000 still holds its bustling *regional market* every first and fourth Sunday of the month and there are a number of excellent affordable restaurants, an example is the *Restaurante Malveiro (Rua*

Fine fairways –
Vale do Lobo golf course

restaurants here serve true gourmet cuisine and are priced accordingly. An example is the Michelin-starred *São Gabriel (lunch Sun, otherwise evenings only | Estrada da Quinta do Lago | tel. 2 89 39 45 21 | www.sao-gabriel.com | Expensive)*, where regional gourmet cuisine is expertly blended with Swiss specialities.

The same goes for the hotels: A right royal experience is how an overnight stay in the *Quinta do Lago (140 rooms and suites | tel. 2 89 35 03 50 | www.hotelquintadolago.com | Expensive)* luxury resort can best be described. Located in a pine forest 5 km/3 miles south-east of Almancil, it offers its guests three 18-hole golf courses. Stately villas surround the *lago*, a freshwater lagoon. It is here where the largely unspoilt the Ria Formosa begins and the view of the dunes and lagoon is breathtaking. The luxury resort 3 km/1.8 miles to the west is *Vale do Lobo (154 rooms and suites | tel. 2 89 35 30 00 | www.valedolobo.com | Expensive)*. The *Ria Park (175 rooms and suites | tel. 2 89 35 98 00 | www.riaparkhotels.com | Moderate–Expensive)* 800 m/2,635 ft from Praia do Garrão is also an enchanting place to stay.

QUARTEIRA
(138 C4–5) (*ॼ K–L7*)
Despite many concrete apartment blocks – telling evidence of misguided development in the Seventies – this city of 16,000 inhabitants is the choice of many Portuguese who want to live in the Algarve. It is no surprise that so many would choose to live here as the city is stretched out along an easily accessible and beautiful sandy beach. The western edge of the city borders on Vilamoura, which seems to have learnt from the development mistakes of its neighbour.

In the area around the **INSIDER TIP** *mercado municipal*, a pretty fish market, you

Vale de Éguas 169 | mobile tel. 9 17 82 41 31 | www.malveiro.com | Moderate), an institution serving Portuguese cuisine with African influences. If you head out towards *Vale do Lobo* and *Quinta do Lago*, several

will find one restaurant after another, serving up really tasty fish dishes at reasonable prices. A seafood lover will feel totally at home at no matter which of the many *marisqueiras* of Quarteira they choose to eat at. The weekly market takes place every Wednesday, the flea market every first Saturday of the month.

VILA REAL DE SANTO ANTÓNIO

(141 F2) (*∅ R5–6*) After the devastating earthquake of 1755 the king decided that he needed to have some form of control over both the trade conducted on the Rio Guadiana and the fishing industry in Monte Gordo.

So King Jose I built the "royal city" of Santo António (previously a small fishing village) in defiance of the Spaniards and to demonstrate the determination of his people. In March 1774 a city plan was drawn up. The city hall was built in August and five months later the city was finished using prefabricated modules – a technique that had also been used when Lisbon was rebuilt.

Sardine and tuna fishing soon brought considerable wealth to this border city and jobs were created thanks to the completion of 45 canning factories. Ironically, the fishermen from nearby Monte Gordo never moved into the houses intended for their use (not even when enforced by the police) because they did not want to live and work under the surveillance of customs authorities. They moved instead to Isla Cristina on the Spanish Atlantic shore.

During the last century the city experienced slump, but today with a population of more than 18,000 it is thriving again – this time it is thanks to tourism. The paved *Praça Marquês de Pombal* forms the proud city centre; from here, the most important shopping streets branch out. The pedestrian zone stretches all the way to the *Avenida da República* along the shore. Plenty of inviting stores are found here, and they are very popular with Spaniards who stream in by ferry from neighbouring Ayamonte or via the motorway bridge. In the shops, customers find an abundance of affordable items such as (beach) towels, blankets and aprons.

FOOD & DRINK

A whole row of restaurants can be found in the extensive pedestrian precinct on the *Avenida da República*. They are all good and reasonably priced. The city's Spanish neighbours have already discovered this and the spectacular waterfront is where they come to hang out.

ASSOCIAÇÃO NAVAL

Stylish atmosphere directly on the Guadiana river, which serves fresh, top quality seafood and has a large selection of tapas. *Av. da República | tel. 2 81 51 30 38 | www. anguadiana.com | Moderate*

ENTERTAINMENT

Monte Gordo is the hub of the city's nightlife. The casino has a relaxed atmosphere. Bars and clubs are open until the early hours.

WHERE TO STAY

Just about all of Santo António's hotels are located in the beach suburb of *Monte Gordo.* Several four-star and three-star hotels (*Moderate–Expensive*) can be found here, including the *Vasco da Gama Hotel (186 rooms and suites | tel. 2 81 51 09 00 | www.vascodagamahotel.com)* and the *Hotel Yellow Praia Monte Gordo (366 Suiten | tel. 2 81 00 89 00 | www.yellowho tels.pt)*, both in the Avenida Infante Dom Henrique. There are attractive offers *(Budget)* to fill the hotel blocks in the off-season, as well as holiday resorts and a camp site.

INFORMATION

POSTO DE TURISMO
Av. Marginal | Monte Gordo | tel. 2 8154 44 95 | www.cm-vrsa.pt

WHERE TO GO

ALCOUTIM ★ (143 F2) *(∅ R2)*
The most enjoyable route to Alcoutim (42 km/26 miles north of Vila Real) leads via Foz de Odeleite through a landscape full of contrasts: There are vineyards, olive groves, fig and apple plantations in the fertile Guadiana valley, which is in stark contrast to the dry and barren land further inland.

Alcoutim (population of 3,500) still retains many of its charms. The *castelo (April–Sept daily 9:30am–7pm, Oct–March 9:30–5:30pm | admission 2.50 euros)* dating back to the 14th century is quite cute. Dating back to the 16th century, the *Igreja Matriz* is also an interesting sight being one of the Algarve's first Renaissance churches. Situated 8 km/5 miles further south, the *Museo do Rio (daily 9:30am–1pm and 2:30–6pm | admission 2,50 euros (joint ticket with other institutions in the region) | Guerreiros do Rio)* provides an insight into the people living on the Rio Guadiana as well as their flora and fauna.

Freshwater swimming in a river dam is an enjoyable activity at the attractive beach of *Praia Fluvial.* Enjoy a meal afterwards on the village square in the restaurant *O Camané (mobile tel. 9 64 10 85 85 | Budget–Moderate)*.

Overnight accommodation in this region is available at the country house *Casa do Vale das Hortas (6 rooms | EN 122 | Vale das Hortas | tel. 2 81 54 70 35 | www.vale dashortas.com | Budget)*.

The event organiser *Fun River (mobile tel. 9 26 68 26 05 | www.fun-river.com)* offers boat trips, hiking tours etc. For more information: *Posto de Turismo (Rua 1° de Maio | Alcoutim | Tel. 2 81 54 61 79 | www. cm-alcoutim.pt)*

CASTRO MARIM ⋙ (141 F2) *(∅ R5)*
In the 14th century this "fort on the coast" was the headquarters for the powerful Order of Christ, which was headed by Prince Henry the Navigator from the beginning of the 15th century. The well preserved ruins of the *castelo* 4 km/2.5 miles north of Vila Real de Santo António are a reminder of a period of great splendour and of a fortress that protected the border to Spain well into the 17th century. These ruins serve as the backdrop to *Dias Medievais* or "medieval days", a fantastic historical festival that takes place at the end of August/beginning of September. The castle parapet gives you a full view of its counterpart *Forte* on a hill nearby (closed to visitors) as well as the Rio Guadiana's expansive estuary and the salines.

MANTA ROTA (141 E3) *(∅ Q6)*
The former fishing village of Manta Rota, 5 km/2.5 miles further south west, has witnessed a transformation similar to Vila Real's suburb *Monte Gordo (141 F3) (∅ R6)*, it has developed into a tourist hotspot with hotel and apartment complexes. Partly enclosed by pine tree forests, the village beaches have remained delightful.

MONTE GORDO (141 F3) (*RG*)

Popular with Dutch tourists and with its own casino and campsite, the holiday town (pop. 2,000) here is spoilt by the concrete hotel blocks yet the resort does offer some interesting points of nature. For example its long stretch of beach with a section reserved as a "parking bay" for fishing boats and **INSIDER TIP** pine forests stretching to the east and west – an excellent spot for walking and jogging.

around the salt marshes. The information centre is reached by taking a 2.2 km/1.4 miles track road on your right along the road to Alcoutim.

TRIPS ALONG THE RIO GUADIANA (141 F1–2, 143 F4–6) (*R3–5*)

A journey along the Rio Guadiana in the direction of Alcoutim is like a journey into another world. The vegetation changes along the way and the area becomes increasingly desolate. The wide valley is

Manta Rota's beach shimmering in the evening light

RESERVA NATURAL DO SAPAL DE CASTRO MARIM (141 E–F2) (*R5–6*)

One of Portugal's most important mudflats lies in the estuary of the Rio Guadiana. Two thirds of the approximately 21 km² (8 square miles) area is covered in water and it is a favoured breeding ground for many aquatic bird species, among them flamingos. Many migratory birds also come here in the winter. Birdwatching is possible near the *information centre* (close to the motorway bridge) and

fertile with olive, orange, lemon and fig groves. The silver ribbon of river will catch your eye all the way to *Mértola*. Its ebb and flow is tidal and the river is especially popular with boat owners because no mooring fees apply. *Riosul (combo tour by boat and jeep 62 euros; including lunch | tel. 2 81510200 | www.riosultravel.com)* offers river rides to music and day jeep tours to Foz de Odeleite and after a hearty lunch it is back by boat to Vila Real.

THE HINTERLAND

The A 22 motorway forms a kind of artificial border between the coast and the hinterland.

Head north and travel to a very different world – the hinterland is tranquil, secluded and pleasantly provincial. The people are friendly; the landscape is hilly with forests, steep terraces, scrubland and pastures, one following the other. The diversity of flora has justifiably earned it the name "Garden of the Algarve".

LOULÉ

★ **(139 D3) *(ØØ L6)* The traditional ways of Loulé (pop. 25,000) are visible in its distinctive market hall with its oriental pink onion domes and windows. Just as pretty: the little old town with its churches, cobbled alleys and a small fortress**.

The longish market hall, which has several entrances, feels almost like an Arabian bazaar. It is a true magnet for visitors and locals alike. There's an additional market with many stalls outside on Saturdays. Around the market you'll find typical restaurants, where you can sit back and watch the pleasant, yet relaxed bustling activity.

Amble around the alleyways and back streets at your leisure and get to know the real Loulé. *Rua da Barbaca* and *Rua da Bica Velha* lead to the *Castelo* and *Igreja Matriz*. The *Rua 5 de Outobro* is a small bustling street full of shops. Remains of the Moorish baths at Largo Dom Pedro I are testimony to Loulé's extensive history; excavation work will still take some years..

Photo: Cork oak trees in the Serra de Monchique

**Secluded and peaceful:
friendly locals and a rural lifestyle
characterise the "Garden of the Algarve"**

Many of the traditional arts and crafts from the Algarve have disappeared – but this doesn't mean they have to be lost altogether. Thanks to local initiatives (such as the one mentioned on p. 19), visitors can learn how to paint tiles or weave with palm. Carnival is a particularly festive time, the celebrations blend pagan and Christian tradition together with an infectious sense of fun that has resulted in Loulé becoming Portugal's most popular place for carnival celebra- In contrast, the religious *Festa da*

Mãe Soberana begins on Easter Sunday and reaches its culmination two weeks later.

SIGHTSEEÎNG

CHURCHES

The *Igreja Matriz* dating from the 13th century is particularly impressive with its *Capela das Almas* covered in *azulejos*, its pillars embellished with floral motifs and a pulpit made of wrought iron. The belfry was once the minaret of a mosque.

Beautiful *azulejos* and gilded carvings are also what make the *Nossa Senhora da Conceição* special. This pilgrimage chapel is located next to the fort. Entry into the hospital *Santa Casa da Misericórdia* on the *Avenida Duarte Pacheco* is through a richly decorated portal, an excellent example of Manueline architecture. The *Correia 17)* can be found inside the fort walls with displays of artefacts from towns like Silves. The local history section in the fort takes you behind the scenes of a typical Algarve kitchen and you can also climb the 🔆 fort tower; everything is included in the admission ticket which you can buy at the museum.

Fresh produce at the weekly market in Loulé

Senhora da Piedade pilgrimage chapel lies on a hill in the direction of Boliqueime. With its modern dome, it looks like a landed UFO. Here the Mãe Soberana (Sublime Virgin Mary) is honoured in the Algarve's biggest religious festival on the second Sunday after Easter.

TOWN WALLS & FORT

Picturesque alleyways wind through the historical town centre to the *castelo* which was built by the Moors in the 12th century. Many parts of the fort and the walls are well preserved and have been partly integrated into newer buildings. A small *Archaeological Museum (Mon–Fri 9:30am–5:30pm, Sat 9:30am–4pm | admission 2 euros | Rua D. Paio Peres*

FOOD & DRINK

CAFÉ CALCINHA

Traditional café from the end of the 1920s in the style of a Brazilian coffee shop. In front of the entrance, the regional poet António Aleixo (1899–1949) sits on a chair cast in bronze. *Closed Sat afternoons, closed Sun | Praça da República 67 | tel. 2 89 41 57 63 | Moderate*

MUSEU DO LAGAR

Pleasant dining on the square in front of the church, small terrace. Specialities include grilled meat dishes, among them black pig. Live music most Fridays. *Closed Sun | Largo Batalhão Sapadores Caminh de Ferro 7 | tel. 2 89 42 27 18 | Mode*

INSIDER TIP **PERDIÇÃO**

Note: The restaurant belonging to the in-genious chef Ana Miguel is open by res-ervation only by phone or e-mail. Ana Miguel, who speaks English very well, then prepares surprise menus for her guests made from regional ingredients. *Rua Camilo Castelo Branco 5A | mobile tel. 919 66 99 53 | perdicao@sapo.pt | Moderate*

SHOPPING

The indoor market hall is a good desti-nation to buy art and craft goods and culinary treats. Carefully hand-painted ceramics can be found in INSIDER TIP *Teresa's Pottery (Largo Dom Pedro I 15 | www.teresapottery.com).*

WHERE TO STAY

INSIDER TIP **LOULÉ CORETO HOSTEL**

Modernised in extremely friendly and vi-brant colours. Affordable prices. Single-sex dorms are available for low-budget travellers. A common kitchen area and roof terrace help guests meet up. Popu-lar among younger travellers especially. *10 rooms | Av. José da Costa Mealha 68 | mobile tel. 966 66 09 43 | loulecoretohos tel.com | Budget*

LOULÉ JARDIM HOTEL

This stylish – and newly renovated – hotel is in a small municipal park in the middle of Loulé. *52 rooms | Largo Manuel d'Arriaga | tel. 289 41 30 94 | www.loulejardimhotel. com | Budget–Moderate*

INFORMATION

POSTO DE TURISMO

Av. 25 de Abril 9 | tel. 289 46 39 00 | www. ᴐ-loule.pt

WHERE TO GO

ALTE (138 B2) (*∅ K5*)

Fig and orange groves surround the town. Secluded picnic spots, a spring fountain, a brook, alleyways and beautiful balcony balustrades decorated with hanging flower pots all give Alte 27 km/17 miles north-west a typical hinterland feel. The town is well known for its astonishingly excessive carnival celebrations.

FONTE DA BENÉMOLA
(139 D2) (*∅ M5*)

Situated 10 km/6 miles north east of Loulé in picturesque rural surroundings is the spring water source of Fonte da Bené-mola with a 4.5 km/2.8 miles circular trail which leads hikers around the area. It can be reached from Querença where other spring water sources are also signposted such as the *Fonte da Barroca* and the site of *Fonte Filipe* which is mentioned in ref-erences dating back to the 12th century.

★ **Loulé**
The market hall and the castle are the must-see sights in this town → p. 74

★ **Serra de Monchique**
The "Garden of the Algarve" goes up all the way to the Fóia (902 m/2,959 ft) → p. 78

★ **Caldas de Monchique**
The Romans loved this spa town which today presents itself mod-ernised → p. 81

★ **Silves**
An imposing Moorish fortress looms large above this tranquil rural town → p. 82

MARCO POLO HIGHLIGHTS

ROCHA DA PENA (138 C1) (*ΩΩ K5*)

Located on a beautiful plateau 20 km/12 miles north of Loulé, this is a hikers' paradise with fascinating old stone ramparts, 120 bird species, and 390 plant species. A circular route starting in the village of *Penina* is where you will begin your adventure in the great outdoors which is not only interesting for bird and plant enthusiasts.

SALIR (138–139 C–D 1–2) (*ΩΩ L5*)

This historic town with a population of 3,500 lies 15 km/9 miles north of Loulé on the N 124. Of the Moorish fort on a hill, all that is visible today are the remnants of a few walls. The area around the hill was occupied as far back as 4,000 years ago. A scenic route takes you from the fort (keep a lookout for eagles that circle over the cork oak and eucalyptus groves) to *Barranco do Velho*, the hub of this rural farmland area. Near Salir, you can find accommodation in the quiet, child-friendly country home **INSIDER TIP** ‣ *Casa da Mãe*

(7 apartments | Almeijoafra | tel. 2 89 48 91 79 | www.casadamae.com | *Budget–Moderate*).

MONCHIQUE & THE SERRA

(133 E6) (*ΩΩ F4*) **The Romans called the central place of the ★ ☙ Serra de Monchique – in the Algarve's highest mountainous terrain – the "Mountain of Flowers" and it lives up to the name with numerous plant species (including many subtropical varieties) flourishing all year round in the "Garden of the Algarve".**

The Serra's unique climatic conditions are ideal for over 1,000 plant species like wild orchids and rhododendrons, peonies, mimosas and in the spring and summer there are masses of blooms everywhere. The sea of colour is absolutely spectacular, as are the views from both of Portugal's

MEDRONHO

Growing wild in the forests of the Serra, the medronho (strawberry) tree is actually like a big bush. The reddish orange colour of its fruit looks very similar to strawberries but its flesh is floury and it smells nothing like a strawberry. Harvesting takes place in November, a laborious task in rough inaccessible terrain and the fruit is often high up. The fruit is stored in wooden barrels until February when the pulpy mixture is fully fermented and ready to be distilled. Everyone in the area lends a hand and there is generally a festive air surrounding the whole process with lots of happy laughter. Steam rising up into the fresh spring air is a sure sign that *medronho* is in the making! Everyone gets to taste the clear fragrant schnapps which, if shaken, makes little pearls on the bottle neck. Tasting is typically accompanied by a slice of Serra ham. Things are not quite as romantic at the professional distilleries – they are subject to strict supervision by the EU. The distilled, strong spirit is silky smooth on the tongue – a national delicacy which is served in all ● restaurants in the Serra.

highest peaks: *Fóia* (902 m/2,959 ft) and *Picota* (773 m/2,536 ft).

A very special experience is taking a drive into the lush green mountain world on the INSIDER TIP road along the *Ribeira de Odelouca* up towards *Alferce* (136 B1) (*m̄ G4*) and on to Monchique. Arriving from the south, you'll see a signpost to Alferce at the village of *Rasmalho*. Take this road and on your way head to *Barragem de Odelouca* (see p. 81), a reservoir with a small carpark and benches from where you can enjoy the view and a picnic.

Strawberry, mimosa, cork oak and chestnut trees are in abundance. There are lots of natural springs and songbirds can be heard twittering wherever you go, while birds of prey can be seen circling above. There are forests, valleys and steep mountain terraces.

Nestled beneath the Fóia is *Monchique,* a small mining and agricultural town with a charming village atmosphere, although it's the most-visited place for Algarve tourists after the Cabo de São Vicente. The soil in the area is particularly fertile thanks to the abundance of water. Of a population of 6,000 more than a sixth are foreigners, making Monchique home to the highest number of foreigners in the whole of Portugal.

Almond blossoms cover the countryside in January and early February

SIGHTSEEING

IGREJA MATRIZ

This church is in constant use by the reverent residents of Monchique but the tourists who visit it are here for a different purpose – its extraordinary Manueline portal. Its naves have columns that are shaped like twisted, knotted rope. Its chestnut wood altar has a statue of *Nossa Senhora da Conceição* dating from the 18th century that is ascribed to sculptor Machado de Castro.

NOSSA SENHORA DO DESTERRO ☀

This 18th century ruined monastery high lies above the city. The 2 km/1.2 mile path from the city centre is not too arduous – and the view is well worth it.

FOOD & DRINK

On the road up to the summit of the Fóia is the town's "food mile" and one thing all the restaurants serve is *frango piri-piri*, a delicious spiced barbecue chicken. It's also worth visiting the hilltop restaurant INSIDER TIP *Jardim das Oliveiras (Sítio do Porto Escuro | tel. 2 82 91 28 74 |*

www.jardimdasoliveiras.com | Moderate), the way is signposted on the road up to Fóia. Surrounded by olive groves, this restaurant is famous for its hearty sausage and meat dishes and, depending on the season, game (wild boar specialty). But the town itself also boasts a number of good restaurants.

A CHARRETTE

Extremely relaxed with real Monchique ambiance and rustic charm. Wild boar, lamb stew, black pig and other Serra de Monchique specialities, and some first class wines are on the menu. The menu is only available in Portuguese, but that can be an adventure in itself. *Rua Dr. Samora Gil 30–34 | next to the City Hall (câmara) | tel. 2 82 91 21 42 | Moderate*

CAFÉ DA VILA

Meeting point on the main square for a coffee or ice cream or even a sandwich, salad or omelette. After your snack, take a stroll along the small pedestrian zone up to the church. *Largo dos Chorões | tel. 2 82 91 23 83 | Budget*

SHOPPING

A variety of quality shops sell ceramics, wooden souvenirs, baskets and leather goods. Their unique folding wooden chairs are a favourite tourist souvenir from the Serra (but you should plan the transport home). They are hand-crafted to a design that can be traced back to the Romans – history's first folding chairs. Not surprising since the Romans were making good use of the nearby hot springs at the resort of Caldas more than 2,000 years ago.

SPORTS & ACTIVITIES

The Serra is an idyllically beautiful area for hiking and cycling – and a vast one. It has an endless network of roads, paths and trails that cover the Fóia and Picota mountains and the valleys. The Via

Recover and relax at the spa resort of Caldas de Monchique

Algarviana hiking trail runs right through it. Wildlife enthusiasts will enjoy the abundant plant life found here and bird lovers will get to see a wide variety of species – from eagles to vultures and bee-eaters to iridescent kingfishers. Cyclists who brave the 902 m/2,959 ft climb up the Fóia will be rewarded with the thrill of coasting down the 35 km/21.7 miles stretch to the sea. Motorists have to be very careful because of all the cyclists on the road!

WHERE TO STAY

BICA-BOA

Irish owners: offering accommodation in four rooms named after the four seasons on the outskirts of Monchique. Furnished in dark wood, it also offers a pleasant terrace. The restaurant serves regional produce, also catering for vegetarians. *Estrada de Lisboa 266 | tel. 2 82 91 22 71 | www.bicaboa.com | Budget*

QUINTA DAS RELVINHAS

Also known as Quinta do Algarve, this stately mansion with its magnificent garden has eight guest rooms and a tepee village. Vast difference in prices; weekly prices are applicable from the start of July to mid-September. Outside the main season, the hotel offers special deals including lodging without board. *Caminho da Fóia | mobile tel. 9 36 43 13 66 | www.quintaalgarve.com | Budget–Moderate*

INFORMATION

POSTO DE TURISMO

Largo de San Sebastião | tel. 2 82 911189 | www.cm-monchique.pt

WHERE TO GO

BARRAGEM DE ODELOUCA

(136–137 B3–D1) *(M G5–H4)*
The dam wall of this reservoir is some 130 m/426 ft long and retains approximately 134 Mio. m³ (47,000 tons) of water. With a depth of 90 m (almost 300 ft) it is the deepest lake of its kind in the Algarve. It stretches all the way to São Marcos da Serra and supplies the whole of the western Algarve – from Sagres to Albufeira – with water. A magnificent panoramic view of the lake can be had from the 🔭 Picota by taking the mountain road 2 km/1.2 mile south of Alferce to the Picota and to Monchique (via Corta Grande).

CALDAS DE MONCHIQUE ★ ●

(136 A2–3) *(M F4)*
This pleasant thermal spa resort lies 5 km/3 miles south of Monchique. These spring waters have been attracting visitors since the Romans started using them to cure rheumatism, skin disorders and respiratory illnesses. Today the Belle Époque-style buildings have been restored and new buildings added. Bubbling from the thermal springs are 2 million litres (440,000 gallons) of water a day and you can relax in 32° C (90° F) temperatures in the *bathhouse.* There are also a sauna and Vichy shower, relaxation and beauty therapy programmes on offer. The spa has five hotels with a total of 102 rooms which are combined under the name *Villa Termal (tel. 2 82 91 09 10 | www.monchiquetermas. com | Moderate).* The water from here is also decanted into bottles and sold as *Água de Monchique* throughout Portugal. Those who don't fancy spending the night here can still enjoy a stroll taking in the fresh air and romantic atmosphere of this resort. Good food can be had at *Wine &*

Beer Bar O Tasco (tel. 2 82 91 09 13 | Budget) and the elegant *Restaurante 1692 (tel. 2 82 91 09 10 | Expensive)* where you can sit outside under its looming trees.

FÓIA ⚘
(136 B2) (*ꭥ F4*)

After the captivating 8 km/5 miles drive from Monchique, you know you have reached the summit when you can see the disconcerting array of aerials and radar units on the 902 m/2,959 ft plateau. But the view from here is brilliant! Throw on a jacket as it can get quite windy. Deserted farms and villages and the remnants of painstaking terracing bear silent testimony to a once thriving agricultural lifestyle. When driving down, after 2 km/3.2 miles stop at the **INSIDER TIP** *Miradouro* viewing point. There is also a spring *(fonte)* where you can get some cool, fresh mountain water.

PICOTA ⚘
(136 B2) (*ꭥ F4*)

The view from this 773 m/2,536 ft granite peak is even more fascinating than that from Fóia. On a clear day you will be able to see the entire coastline all the way to Sagres as well as the series of hills rolling towards the coast. If you turn your back to the coast view, you will see the magnificent, deserted Alentejo region. How to get there: from Monchique drive towards Alferce, then turn off immediately and head up. The way to the summit is signposted. While away some time sitting on the granite rocks on this quiet peak – there is no pub, or restaurant, so remember to bring a picnic. There are countless eucalyptus trees on the slopes.

SILVES

(136 C4) (*ꭥ G 5–6*) **Under the control of the Moors *Xelb* – which later became** ★ **Silves – was a magnificent metropolis full of palaces and bazaars. At the height of its power it was considered to be on a par with Granada and even more important than Lisbon.**

A powerful reminder of its heyday is its imposing castle fortress that can be seen from a distance – the crenelated red sandstone wall around it glows in the sunlight. The locals say that Silves has the country's "warmest light". The Silves orange groves also date back to the days of the Moors, as do the ruins of its old wells *(noras)*. At that time the Rio Arade was navigable all the way to Silves. The waterway has long since become silted up.

Contemporary art in the historical capital of the Moors: market square in Silves

Today Silves with its population of 11,000 is a tranquil, very engaging small rural town with plenty of charm, surrounded by orange plantations. The restored market hall *(mercado municipal)* is closed only on Sundays and a good meeting place. This otherwise tranquil town comes to life once a year for its week-long medieval festival, the *Feira Medieval*, held mid-August with an impressive program of events. The landmark in the lower part of the city is its extensive esplanade with pools and modern works of sculpture. Be prepared to break out into a sweat on the way up to the *castelo*.

SIGHTSEEING

CASTELO ☆

Imposing is the only word to describe this citadel fortress – seven sections of wall surrounding some 3 acres of land and twelve fortified towers and ramparts that made it virtually impregnable in its day. Its cisterns have since become exposed (the biggest one is more than 60 m/200 ft deep), also the vaults that once served as escape routes. The restorers seem to have been a bit over-eager in some places. The *castelo (summer 9am–6:30pm, winter 9am–5pm | admission 2.80 euros, jooint ticket with the Archaeological Museum 3.90 euros)* was thought to have been built on top of the remnants of a Roman or Visigoth fort. In their tributes to the structure, Moor poets called it the "Palace of the Verandas". The city walls that once extended from the fort walls are no more – razed to the ground by Christian conquerors. There is a wonderful view from the castle hill.

Silves' castelo built between the 9th and 12th century and restored in the Forties

MUSEU MUNICIPAL DE ARQUEOLOGIA

The archaeological museum is located 200 m/656 ft in the direction of the town. Finds dating from the Stone Age era through to medieval times are exhibited here, including some beautiful Arabic ceramics. The descent into a 20 m/65 ft deep Moorish well shaft is fascinating. *Daily 10am–6pm | admission 2.10 euros, joint ticket with the castle 3.90 euros*

SÉ

Jutting up between the fortress and the rural town is the Algarve's oldest Christian church building, the Sé cathedral. When Silves was conquered for the second time by the Christians in 1242, it was built on top of the ruins of a mosque using the local red sandstone. After its devastation in the earthquake of 1755 the locals rebuilt some parts, but this time in the baroque style. *Mon–Fri 9am–1pm and 2–6pm, Sat 9am–1pm | admission 1 euro*

FOOD & DRINK

O ALAMBIQUE

This restaurant in the village of *Poço Barreto* 3 km/1.8 mile outside town on the road to Alcantarilha is a magnet for international tourists. *Open evenings only, closed Tuesdays | tel. 2 82 44 92 83 | Moderate–Expensive*

O BARRADAS

Andrea Pequeno is a master chef; husband Luís is at her side. Excellent cuisine. Oven-prepared seafood dishes are their speciality – especially their fish baked in salt. *Evenings only, closed Wed | Venda Nova (2 km/1.2 mile to the south)| tel. 2 82 44 33 08 | www.obarradas.com | Moderate*

CAFÉ INGLÊS ☆

An evergreen. Enjoy an oven-fired pizza, a salad or a slice of homemade cake this café situated high above the tow the foot of the fort. Fri and Sat from 8.30pm, Sun from 2:30pm with live music. *Rua do Castelo 11 | tel. 2 82 44 25 85 | www.cafeingles.com.pt | Moderate*

SPORTS & ACTIVITIES

Aside from travelling by bus, rail or car, you can also visit Silves by taking a boat ride on the *Rio Arade* from *Portimão's Cais Vasco da Gama | Duration approx. 1–2 hours depending on the tide*

WHERE TO STAY

INSIDER TIP CASA DAS OLIVEIRAS

Family-run guest house surrounded by vineyards and orange groves 6 km/3.7 miles from Silves en route to Lagoa. Friendly atmosphere, five lovely rooms, pool, very tranquil setting. *Tel. 2 82 34 21 15 | www.casa-das-oliveiras.com | Budget*

COLINA DOS MOUROS ☆

The only major hotel in Silves, it is ideally located in the valley with views of the fortress and just 300 m/984 ft from the centre of town across the Roman bridge. *73 rooms | near the Rotunda Cruz de Portugal | tel. 2 82 34 04 70 | www.colina-hotels.com | Moderate*

QUINTA DA FIGUEIRINHA ☆ ⊙

A 36 acre organic fruit and vegetable farm with nine apartments, a pool and views of the Monchique mountains. *Turn left on the road that takes you to Faro and travel for a further 5 km/3 miles | tel. 2 82 44 07 00 | www.qdf.pt | Budget*

INFORMATION

STO DE TURISMO

e EN 124 | tel. 2 82 44 22 55 | www. es.pt

WHERE TO GO

ALGOZ (137 E5) (⫘ J6)

This tranquil provincial village – tucked away from the hustle and bustle – is 14 km/8.6 miles east of Silves. Close by it on the road to Ferreiras you will find *Quinta dos Avós (Wed–Mon 2–7pm | www.quintadosavos.pt)* which specialises in traditional medieval monastery desserts and a whole variety of herbal teas. The owners also run the museum *Museu Rural* next door which displays horse carriages.

On the southern border of the village lies the romantic windmill estate ☆ INSIDER TIP *Moinho do Pedro (4 rooms, 2 apartments, 1 suite | tel. 2 82 57 54 69 | www.moinhodopedro.com | Budget–Moderate)* dating back to the 17th century. It has a Mediterranean feel to it and a spectacular view all the way to the sea. A bar, sauna and various spa programmes are also on offer.

BARRAGEM DO ARADE & BARRAGEM DO FUNCHO

(137 D–E 2–3) (⫘ H4–5)

6 km/3.7 miles east of Silves turn in the direction of *Barragem do Arade*, drive on 3 km/1.8 mile further and just before you reach the dam wall turn left to the *Arade lake*. Even more impressive is Funcho lake which is slightly higher. So instead of turning off to Barragem do Arade, turn right just before the dam wall, then 3 km/1.8 mile further on you will see a sign in *Vale Fuzeiros* saying *Barragem do Funcho*. Drive down the road for a further 3 km/1.8 mile and you will come upon the isolated world of the Serra and *lake Funcho*. If you are travelling there in the height of summer best to come prepared, as there is little shade. South-east of the lake lies the tiny authentic rural village of *São Bartolomeu de Messines*.

THE WEST COAST

The entire length of the Costa Vicentina is a nature reserve. A landscape that rises from sea level to a height of 900 m/2,952 ft in the Serra de Monchique. There are valleys, lagoons, magnificent cliffs and pristine rivers.

In spite of the fact that its tourism infrastructure is quite limited, there are many individualists who are fans of the region – so it is best to book well in advance. But the wild, romantic charms of Europe's most south westerly coast can also be discovered on a day trip.

ALJEZUR

(132 B6) (*D4*) This tranquil small town is the shopping and municipal hub of the sparsely populated coastal region. Only 5,300 people live in the entire administrative district.

The atmosphere here is very quiet and relaxed as everywhere on the west coast. Farmers, villagers and townspeople live in friendly harmony with settlers from other parts of Europe. Aljezur (pronounced: al-shay-zoor) on the river *Ribeira de Aljezur* makes for a good starting point to explore the west coast, especially for hikers: on the GR-11 trail it's 12 km/7.5 miles to Arrifana and 18 km/11 miles to Odeceixe.

SIGHTSEEING

CASTELO ☆
Perched at the top of the hill is the

Photo: Beach along the Costa Vicentina

Experience unspoilt landscapes: on the wild and romantic west coast, you've come to just the right place

ruin of a Moorish castle, accessible for free at all times and not renovated. Crusaders conquered the castle in the middle of the 13th century. It is a short ten minute climb from the lower part of town but well worth every step for the stunning panoramic view, but you can also drive up by car. The small *Museu de Arte Sacra* is situated next to the parish church on the way to the castle; it exhibits ecclesiastical art.

The first floor welcomes visitors with its local history exhibition of hoes, axes, weaving looms, rowing boats; the museum also features a tiny kitchen. *Tue–Sat 9am–1pm and 2–5pm (in the summer until 6pm) | admission 2 euros | Largo 5 de Outobro*

FOOD & DRINK

CAFÉ DO MERCADO
Small café next to the indoor market hall where you can purchase the freshest produce. Ideal for a stop in between. *Largo do Mercado | Budget*

The beautiful Praia da Arrifana at the foot of Ponta Arrifana

PONT'A PÉ
This cosy restaurant, café and bar is a stone's throw from the river and ha s become the town's favourite. Good hearty food. Some seats on the terrace. *Closed Sun | Largo de Liberdade 12 | tel. 2 82 99 81 04 | www.pontape.pt | Budget*

WHERE TO STAY

AMAZIGH HOSTEL
Popular traveller's destination especially because of its cheap prices. Those on a low-budget can opt to sleep in the dorm instead of the private rooms. *10 rooms, 2 dorms with 24 beds each | Rua da Ladeira 5 | tel. 2 82 99 75 02 | www.amazighostel.com | Budget*

CASA CALENDULA
Three comfortable houses each accommodating two to four people. It is near to Praia da Amoreira and set in a large park surrounded by nature. House prices don't include final cleaning. *Tel. 2 82 99 84 27 | www.casa-calendula.com | Budget–Moderate*

INFORMATION

POSTO DE TURISMO
Rua 25 do Abril 62 | tel. 2 82 99 82 29 | www.cm-aljezur.pt

WHERE TO GO

ARRIFANA ★ (134 B1) (*m C4*)
About 1 km/0.6 mile south of Aljezur the road branches off to the village of *Monte Clérigo* with its colourful wooden houses and its expansive beach. You can get a good meal at the small *O Zé (tel. 2 82 99 86 21 | Budget–Moderate)* restaurant, which is right on the beach and serves excellent seafood. Afterwards take a drive along the road by the dunes towards *Vale da Telha* and then on to *Arrifana*, 15 km/9 miles from Aljezur. Set on a crescent shaped bay, this tow is increasingly popular with surfers a

the view of the steep coastline from the ruin of the fort on the *Ponta da Arrifana* cliff is magnificent. Its origins date back to 1635. ● This is where you should have your picnic. You will get the full panoramic view of the bay in the south and the gigantic cliff faces all the way to Ponta de Atalaia in the north. Heavenly at sunset! For those not inclined to take a picnic, there is a good restaurant right in front of the Fortaleza specialising in seafood, INSIDER TIP *Restaurante O Paulo (closed Mon | tel. 282995184 | www.restauranteopaulo.com | Moderate)* with its big panorama windows.

ODECEIXE (132 B4) (*D3*)

This town lies 16 km/10 miles north of Aljezur on the small river of Seixe. In the late afternoon its many restaurants become packed (the food here is tasty and reasonably priced) and before you know it all the tables on the street will be taken, especially those surrounding the *Largo 1 Maio* square. The place is relatively unsophisticated and the absence of glamour is quite refreshing. Odeceixe is connected to the long-distance hiking trail *Rota Vicentina* which is well signposted.

he *Praia de Odeceixe* sandy beach stretches out 2 km/1.2 mile west of the main town. Both the north and the south of the Seixe estuary are flanked by steep cliffs. The road south of the bay takes you past cliff headlands where white storks quietly breed undeterred by the sea spray. An excellent base for exploring the entire region is the INSIDER TIP *Reguengos holiday resort (6 rooms, 4 apartments, 1 bungalow | tel. 282911901 | Budget–Moderate)* which has unsophisticated accommodation in ecological wood houses. There are lots of activities designed to relax and rejuvenate like yoga and massages.

CABO DE SÃO VICENTE

(134 A6) (*B7*) From Sagres the road takes you along a wind-swept headland though a spectacular landscape to continental Europe's most south-westerly point. This superlative alone makes the trip worthwile. The ★ Cabo de São Vicente is the Algarve's most visited destination.

MARCO POLO HIGHLIGHTS

★ Arrifana
Spectacular view of the crescent-shaped bay and the steep rocky coast → p. 88

★ Cabo de São Vicente
Europe's most south-westerly cape swept by wind and waves → p. 89

Here you will experience the elements – wind and water – up close and personal. On some days the sea spray from the breakers crashing against the rocks will shoot hundreds of feet into the air above the cliffs. Clinging to a rock, with the sea raging below, is a bright red and white 150 year-old 24 m/78 ft ☀ lighthouse which seems to a stand in defiance instruments yet the main fascination here is the unbeatable views across the Atlantic and cliffs. Warning: do not venture too close to the cliff edge as there have been fatal casualties here in the past! The car park in front of the cape is a bustling location full of fast-food and souvenir stands.

The Cabo de São Vicente lighthouse beacon is the Atlantic's most powerful

house which seems to a stand in defiance of the deserted bleakness of the area. Its 3,000 watt beacon is visible almost 90 km/55 miles away and is far superior to any others on the Atlantic coast. Numerous naval battles were fought in the vicinity of this strategically important cape between the 17th and 19th centuries. Situated on the lighthouse's forecourt, a small *museum* open to the public exhibits its model ships of caravels and nautical On the return journey to Sagres you can pay a visit to the remains of the *Santa Catarina* fortress. The complex is on a dramatically beautiful cliff above a bay. In its heyday Prince Henry the Navigator had his headquarters here according to historians who are also convinced that the round *Santa Catarina* chapel represents the last remains of this "princely town" (Vila d' Infante).

A more worthwhile stop is the car park above the **INSIDER TIP** *Praia de Beliche*, a secluded beach paradise to be reached down a set of stairs; the beach is also a popular spot for surfers.

WHERE TO GO

CARRAPATEIRA & SURROUNDINGS

The 🌿 *Costa Vicentina* coastal trail will take you from the cape to Odeceixe. Hikers along this stretch will probably not come across anyone else en route. Far below the road, the waves crash on to the reefs and on to the weathered white cliffs. There are magnificent views everywhere you look. Nestled down between the mighty cliff faces of this wild landscape are some tranquil sandy bays.

The entire stretch all the way until *Carrapateira* 28 km/17 miles north of Cabo de São Vicente, is captivating. 10 km/6 miles walk away to the north of the cape is *Torre de Aspa* (134 A5) (f B7) with its 🌿 *Miradouro da Grota*, offering splendid views over the cliffs and surrounded by flowering cistus. It is advisable to take a guided tour on foot organised by the English-speaking tour guide Nicolau da Costa *Atalaia Walking* (see p. 111) who knows this region (and its dangers) like the back of his hand.

The *Praia do Castelejo* and *Praia da Cordoama* beaches in Vila do Bispo and a few kilometres further north the *Praia da Bordeira* (with lagoon) and *Praia do Amado* (134 B3) (💭 C6) are beautiful. The Praia do Amado is the most well-known surfing beach around, several surf schools (see p. 111) offer courses here. You can eat well at the *Sítio do Rio (Praia da Bordeira | tel. 2 82 97 31 19 | Budget)*. Try the *perceves*!

* recommended accommodation option *Carrapateira* (134 B3) (💭 C5–6) itself

is the cosy country-style guest house *Das Dunas (4 rooms and 6 apartments | Rua da Padaria 9 | tel. 2 82 97 31 18 | www.pensao-das-dunas.pt | Budget)*.

The small village of **INSIDER TIP** *Pedralva* (134 C4) (💭 C6) (Tel. 2 82 63 93 42 | www.aldeiadapedralva.com)*, approximately 10 km/6 miles north of Vila do Bispo, is busy experiencing a Renaissance of sorts with alternative tourism such as nature hikes. Here you can rent a wide range of renovated village houses with varying facilities *(Moderate–Expensive)*. There are a total of 25 houses to choose from. Yet this village is worth a brief stop even if only to stroll around its picturesque streets or stop for a bite to eat at *Café Central (Budget)*, *Pizza Pazza (Budget–Moderate)*, which is known for its excellent pizzas, and the Restaurante *Sítio da Pedralva (Moderate–Expensive)*.

DISCOVERY TOURS

1 ALGARVE AT A GLANCE

START: ❶ Faro
END: ❶ Faro

Distance:
🚗 580 km/360 miles

11 days
Driving time
(without stops)
12.5 hours

COSTS: 1,000 euros per person for accommodation, food, rental car, petrol, toll, admissions and boat tour
WHAT TO PACK: swimwear, sun protection

IMPORTANT TIPS: Pre-book your hotel accommodation in summer. When you start the tour in Faro, directly book a hotel room for your final day.
When hiring the rental car, remember the automatic toll system for the motorways → p. 121.
It is difficult to find parking spaces close to beaches in summer.

Every corner of the earth has its own special charm. If you want to explore all the many different facets of this region, head off the beaten track or get tips for the best stops, breathtaking views, hand-picked restaurants or the best local activities, then these customised discovery tours are just the right thing. Choose the best route for the day and follow in the footsteps of the MARCO POLO authors – well-prepared to navigate your way to all the many highlights that await you along the tour.

Experience all the many facets of the Algarve on this extensive tour of the region. It takes you to the region's beaches and cliffs, its most rewarding cities, harbours and also further inland for you to see another side of the Algarve. The tour starts and ends at Faro airport where you can collect your rental car and discover this splendid city. Your journey first takes you east and then continues to the far west of the region. Remember to give yourself enough time to swim, take relaxing breaks in bars and beach restaurants and explore the region on nature tours.

Start your holiday the Latin way: Once you have arrived
n Faro by plane and collected your rental car, it's time to

DAY 1

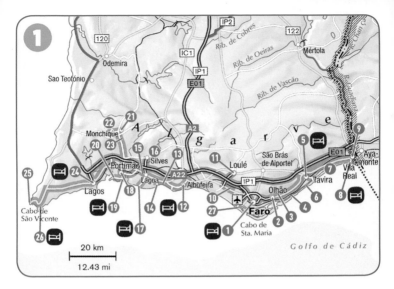

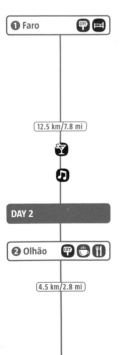

❶ Faro 🍷 🏨

12.5 km / 7.8 mi

🍸

🎵

DAY 2

❷ Olhão 🍷 ☕ 🍴

4.5 km / 2.8 mi

relax and enjoy the region's flair by first visiting the city of **❶ Faro → p. 56.** Anything but a stop en-route and expressionless sea of houses, Algarve's metropolis offers far more. Although it takes some time to reach its picturesque harbour and the **Old Town p. 59 (on signposts it is called Vila-Adentro),** you'll be pleasantly surprised when you finally arrive. Once you have checked into your hotel, immerse yourself in the historical quarter with its narrow streets and cathedral inside the fully-intact high city walls. The best spot to watch the sunset over the city is near the Largo do Castelo, the **O Castelo → p. 59,** where you may also catch some live music. If you ask a local about the city's nightlife, they will point you in the direction of the **Rua do Crime!**

The first stop of the day **on the N 125 coastal road** is the small port town of **❷ Olhão → p. 62** with the Algarve's most charming **fish market** in one of the town's two indoor market halls. Plan to arrive here at lunchtime at the latest to experience the market's flair and smells. First enjoy a refreshment in one of the cafés situated between the two market buildings and then head to the traditional fish restaurant **O Bote** (daily | Av. 5 de Outoubro | tel. 2 89 72 11 83 | Moderate). After a hearty lunch, it's time to burn off the calories on the 4 km/2.5 miles picturesque circular trail through a small section of the **Ria Formosa → p. 64** nature reserve. The route starts next to the visitors' centre ❸ **Quinta de Marim → p. 114**, the road turnoff to the centre **is signposted from the N 125 to Tavira, 1 km/0.6 mile to the east of Olhão, with the brown sign "Ria Formosa". Back on the N 125 national road, now follow the second signposted stop to** ❹ **Fuseta → p. 66**. Highlights here include the small port and the lagoon beach. For quick refreshment, stop at the bar close to the port entrance **INSIDER TIP** **O Farol** (daily | Rua Professor César Oliveira | mobile tel. 9 36 06 43 69 | Budget). Today's overnight stop is ❺ **Tavira → p. 63**, one of the most scenic towns in the Algarve and once the region's capital with a flourishing port. The town invested its wealth in churches – well over twenty of them in total. Tavira is still known today as the town of churches and chapels even though it struggles to fill them with young priests.

Take your time today to discover the beauties of Tavira. A particular art historian highlight amongst the many churches is the **Igreja da Misericórdia → p. 64**, while the upper part of the town offers a small **castle → p. 64** with a splendid view and a panoramic 360 degrees view can be seen from the **camera obscura → p. 63** in the former water tower. The zone of restaurants stretches from the former indoor market to the Praça da República and continues on the other side of the river w**hich you cross from the pedestrian-only Roman bridge.** A trip over to the island ❻ **Ilha de Tavira → p. 66** with its fabulous beach is also recommended at some part of the day – a shuttle boat service is available directly from the town centre during the summer months.

Now head east to Monte Gordo. On the way, the hamlet of ❼ **Cacela Velha → p. 66** situated on top of the hill is worth a stop offering fantastic views over the lagoon landscape of the Ria Formosa. While you are here, aim to see the village's **church** and the traditional Algarve **cemetery**. The restaurant **Casa Velha** (closed Mon | tel. 2 81 95 22 97 | Budget–Moderate) is a pleasant spot for a bite to eat which you cannot miss on entering the village. Although ❽ **Monte Gordo → p. 73** is a built-up suburb, its wide sandy beach is very convincing and worth a stop for a swim before checking in to one of the town's many hotels, for example the **Vasco da Gama**

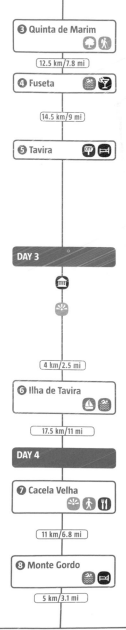

❸ Quinta de Marim

12.5 km/7.8 mi

❹ Fuseta

14.5 km/9 mi

❺ Tavira

DAY 3

4 km/2.5 mi

❻ Ilha de Tavira

17.5 km/11 mi

DAY 4

❼ Cacela Velha

11 km/6.8 mi

❽ Monte Gordo

5 km/3.1 mi

Inside and outside the market hall: market day in Loulé is a colourful event

⑨ Vila Real de Santo António 📱🛍️🍴

Hotel → p. 72. Your last destination in the Eastern Algarve is **⑨ Vila Real de Santo António → p. 71**, a lively commercial town with a promenade directly on the shores of the Rio Guadiana and definitely worth a stay with an evening meal here before **returning the few kilometres to Monte Gordo** where you can rest your weary body...

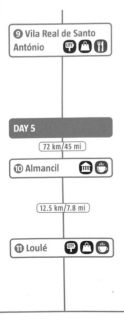

DAY 5

72 km/45 mi

⑩ Almancil 🏛️☕

12.5 km/7.8 mi

⑪ Loulé 📱🛍️☕

Now you have discovered the eastern part of the Algarve, a journey back along the same route would be rather unspectacular so **from Vila Real de Santo António, take the A 22 motorway instead to the exit ⑩ Almancil → p. 69** where you can visit the cultural site **Igreja de São Lourenço → p. 69**, an absolutely delightful church adorned with azulejos tiles! **Pastelaria São Lourenço** opposite the church offers a delicious selection of cakes and pastries to keep you going. Now head inland **on the N 125 and N 396** to the small town of **⑪ Loulé → p. 74**, where you should try and arrive for lunch to take a stroll around its **indoor market hall,** a lively and colourful place where traders s only the freshest produce. The town's outdoor mark held on Saturdays where it seems half the Algarve comes to hunt for the best bargains. The small **castle complex** and chapel **Nossa Senhora da Conceição** are also worth visiting in Loulé. If you need a break, head for the traditional **Café Calcinha → p. 76** on the main square. **Now head back to the N 396 and then along the N 125 and N 395** towards the coast as it's now time to hit the sea and the main tourist destination of ⑫ **Albufeira → p. 32.** The best accommodation can be found in the east along the Praia da Falesia beach. There is always something going on in the lively centre of Albufeira, especially in the evenings.

As there is no direct coastal road from Albufeira **heading to the faraway west,** your route now winds past cliffs and beaches and takes you surprisingly far inland. You'll pass by charming beaches on this stretch, the **Praia da Galé** and the ⑬ **Praia Grande** before you reach Armação de Pêra → p. 36. Now it's definitely time to take a plunge here! Inland close to the Praia Grande stretches the **Lagoa dos Salgados,** a lake perfect for bird-watching. To the west of Armação de Pêra you'll notice the chapel of ⑭ **Nossa Senhora da Rocha → p. 37** perched on the edge of a cliff over the sea. The view alone is worth the visit – and at the foot of the cliffs are splendid beaches on both sides. **Drive along the N 125 until you reach the small inland town of Lagoa → p. 51.** It is home to a **wine cooperative** and the art gallery **Arte Algarve → p. 51** – both situated in the same large building ⑮ **Edificio Adega de Lagoa** directly on the main thoroughfare: a successful combination and worth a stop if only to purchase some cheap, good-quality wine. From Lagoa, **veer off your main route slightly by heading north on the N124–1** to ⑯ **Silves → p. 82,** the former stronghold of the Moors and still overlooked by the majestic red sandstone castle on top of the hill which can be seen from far; this former splendour has been extensively restored.

That was the last cultural destination for today so drive **straight back to the coast through Lagoa** to the classic beachside resorts of ⑰ **Carvoeiro → p. 49** and the **Praia do Carvoeiro** where you will spend the night and have a last chance for a splash in the waves. There is no shortage of bars and cafes here. A popular meeting point directly behind the main beach is the **Grand Café** (daily) or you head slightly inland to the **Restaurant Stone Steak**

31.5 km/19.6 mi

⑫ Albufeira

DAY 6

28.5 km/17.5 mi

⑬ Praia Grande

5 km/3.1 mi

⑭ Nossa Senhora da Rocha

9.5 km/5.9 mi

⑮ Edificio Adega de Lagoa

10.5 km/6.5 mi

⑯ Silves

12 km/7.5 mi

⑰ Carvoeiro

16.5 km/10 mi

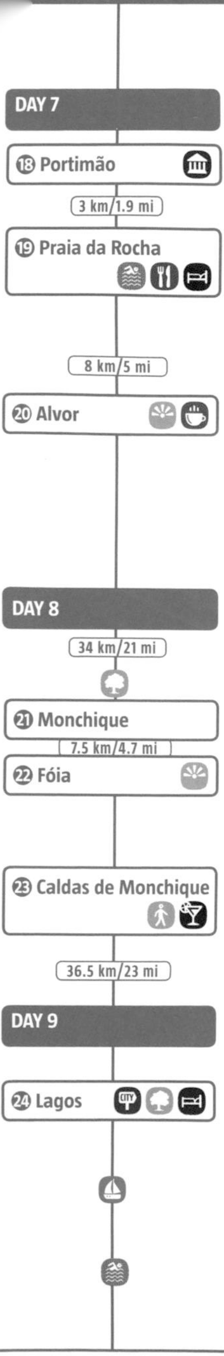
DAY 7
18 Portimão
3 km/1.9 mi
19 Praia da Rocha
8 km/5 mi
20 Alvor
DAY 8
34 km/21 mi
21 Monchique
7.5 km/4.7 mi
22 Fóia
23 Caldas de Monchique
36.5 km/23 mi
DAY 9
24 Lagos
CITY

(closed Mon | Monte Carvoeiro | tel. 282357730 | Moderate), which serves mainly meat dishes.

Drive inland past Lagoa to the town of ⑱ **Portimão → p. 44** on the Arade River where you can visit the **Museu Municipal → p. 45** situated in a former fish-canning factory. Located west of the mouth of the Rio Arade, the coastal suburb ⑲ **Praia da Rocha → p. 51** has a fantastic beach which is what attracts most tourists; soak up the atmosphere here outside one of the beach restaurants such as **Portimão** *(daily | directly on the beach | tel. 282423422 | Moderate)* before or after a dip in the sea. The large choice of hotels makes it worth staying the night and planning a brief excursion to ⑳ **Alvor → p. 49 just a few kilometres west.** The promenade is a popular spot with a view out onto the vast estuary and marshlands of the Ria de Alvor→ p. 49. **Café na Ria** *(daily | Zona Ribeirinha | tel. 282415559 | Budget)* offers a lively outdoor terrace however nothing in comparison to the nightlife in Praia da Rocha.

Today's agenda takes you to the Serra de Monchique → p. 78, a mountain range sometimes hidden away in the clouds. **Climbing north along the N 124 and N 266,** stop for a break in the town of ㉑ **Monchique → p. 78**, just a few kilometres away from the peak of the Algarve: With an elevation of 902 m/2,959 ft, ㉒ **Fóia → p. 82** is the region's highest mountain. Luckily its fantastic panoramic views compensate for the sober summit topped by antennas. **Take the same route back** with a well-earned relaxation in the historical spa resort of ㉓ **Caldas de Monchique → p. 81** where you can stretch your legs and have a drink in the **Wine & Beer Bar O Tasco → p. 81** right in the village centre.

The route now winds inland on the N 125 from Praia da Rocha to ㉔ **Lagos → p. 39**, your next port of call. Lagos is not the place if you are in a rush as it takes time to discover the city, its squares and the **Ponta da Piedade → p. 40** The wind and waves have chiselled out unusual cliff formations along this stretch of coastline. Take a **boat tour → p. 42** from the marina to admire the Ponta da Piedade from out at sea. Now it's your chance to cool down by heading to the largest beach which is situated east of the town: **Meia Praia → p. 42**.

That the Algarve is a region of many facets becomes clear when you drive **from Lagos along the N 125 to ㉕ Cabo de São Vicente → p. 89,** Portugal's most south-westerly point. Even from a distance, the lighthouse marks the way and there are grandiose views over the cliffs with smells of the sea and far-away places. Spend the night in ㉖ Sa-gres → p. 51, a picturesque harbour town which boasts a fortress and surrounding beaches.

Don't just see this last day as your journey home **that brings you back to Faro along the N 125 and then the A 22 motorway. Take the signposted way to the "Aero-porto", past the airport** and head to ㉗ Ilha de Faro. **Follow the signs to the island along the water's edge down a narrow one-way street** signalled by traffic lights. Park up at the end of this street to take a dip in the sea on the other side of this narrow island or a stroll along the beach. Finish the day and your tour of the Algarve in style in ❶ Faro → p. 56 on the restaurant terrace of Pa-quete *(closed Tue | Av. Nascente 16 | tel. 289817760 | Budget–Moderate)* where you can enjoy fish dishes and the beach view.

DAY 10

| 56.5 km/35 mi |

㉕ Cabo de São Vicente

| 7 km/4.3 mi |

㉖ Sagres

DAY 11

| 121 km/75 mi |

㉗ Ilha de Faro

| 9 km/5.6 mi |

❶ Faro

2 AT ONE WITH NATURE: THE WILD WEST

START: ❶ Lagos	1 day
END: ❽ Salema	Driving time
Distance:	(without stops)
➡ 130 km/80 miles	4,5 hours

COSTS: 60 euros per person for rental car, petrol, food
WHAT TO PACK: sun protection, swimwear, water to drink

IMPORTANT TIPS: Traffic can be slow moving along certain sections such as the tracks down to the beaches; hence the long driving time. Pre-book the rental car.
Be careful when swimming in the Atlantic due to the strong currents and waves.

Desolate, wild and untouched – this tour focuses on the Algarve's coastal nature with amazing views over cliffs chiselled out by the wind and waves. Starting in La-s through the Algarve's inland to the west coast, the route then heads to the wil-ess of Portugal's south-westerly point and lands on the gentler southern coast.

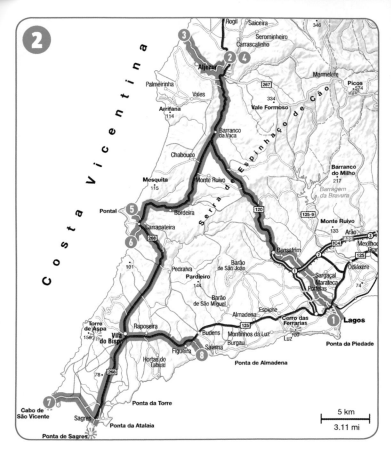

❶ Lagos

32.5 km / 20 mi

❷ Aljezur 🏰 🏛 ☕

09:00am From ❶ Lagos → p. 39 **take the N 120 North West towards Bensafrim** and you will soon encounter fertile agricultural land in varying shades of green dotted with orange and lemon trees – definitely a stark contrast to the Algarve's coastal landscape! Leaving the transit town of Bensafrim behind you, the N 120 takes you up and down through scrub land and past eucalyptus, pine and holm oak trees until you meet the main road from Sagres on your left – your first destination for today is ❷ **Aljezur** → p. 86. The **castelo** above Aljezur catches your gaze immediately. **Take the steep uphill driveway** up to the castle ruins which are open to the public and present you wi[th] a fantastic panoramic view. Return to the lower par[t] the village, **cross the river** and take an immediate left to the small **indoor market hall** *(closed Sun)*. Make your purchases before heading to the market cafe **Café do Mercado** for refreshment.

11:30am Now it's time to drive to Costa Vicentina. **Just a few kilometres north west of Aljezur,** the ❸ **Praia da Amoreira** (signposted turnoff) stretches out and is admired by both locals and visitors as one of Portugal's most captivating bays on the west coast. At the bay's northerly point stands a black rock, known as the "lying man", due to its perpendicular layers of rock sculpted by nature's forces. Now's your chance to take a plunge in the Atlantic followed by a well-earned meal back in Aljezur with a bit of luck on the riverside restaurant terrace of ❹ **Pont'a Pé** → p. 88.

03:00pm After your meal, **take the N 268 heading south from Aljezur,** a sparsely populated region through a mountain range where isolated farmhouses have long been left deserted. You will reach Bordeira on your left but carry on to the next town of **Carrapateira → p. 91. Take a right down to** ❺ **Praia da Bordeira** where sand dunes separate a lagoon from the sea. Here you can try out the special and energetic sport of **INSIDER TIP** Beachwalking by wading through the waters behind the car park. **Drive back to Carrapateira, then, at the road heading to Vila do Bispo, take the road to the right to the signposted** ❻ **Praia do Amado**, a fantastic beach for surfers and home to surfing schools such as the **Future Surfing School** *(mobile tel.*

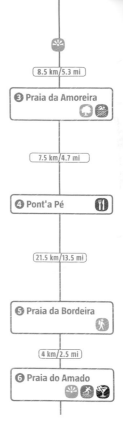

8.5 km/5.3 mi

❸ Praia da Amoreira

7.5 km/4.7 mi

❹ Pont'a Pé

21.5 km/13.5 mi

❺ Praia da Bordeira

4 km/2.5 mi

❻ Praia do Amado

A treat for experienced swimmers: breaking waves on the Praia da Bordeira

9 18 75 58 23 | www.future-surf.com) You can admire the panorama here in any event – with or without a surfing board. Refreshment is also available during the season at the bar on the way down to the beach.

`06:00pm` **Back on the main road, drive through Vila do Bispo and the fortress and port town of** Sagres→ p. 51 to **❼ Cabo de São Vicente → p. 89.** The rugged coastal panorama around the lighthouse is unrivalled with the sea below you gurgling, foaming and spitting. The afternoon sun also adds to this particularly unique setting. Finish your tour by **driving off the N 125 for a last detour to Portugal's southern coast.** Your destination is **❽ Salema** with its splendid beach. Slowly unwind here by taking a dip in the Atlantic or a bite to eat in one of the town's bars and restaurants. **Boia → p. 44** offers a special location over the beach of Salema.

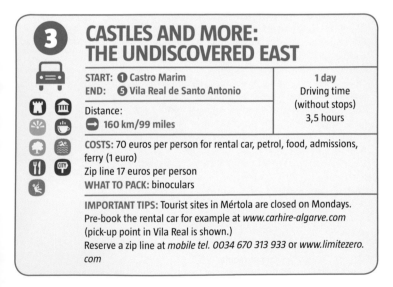

❸ CASTLES AND MORE: THE UNDISCOVERED EAST

START: ❶ Castro Marim	1 day
END: ❺ Vila Real de Santo Antonio	Driving time (without stops)
Distance: ➡ 160 km/99 miles	3,5 hours

COSTS: 70 euros per person for rental car, petrol, food, admissions, ferry (1 euro)
Zip line 17 euros per person
WHAT TO PACK: binoculars

IMPORTANT TIPS: Tourist sites in Mértola are closed on Mondays. Pre-book the rental car for example at *www.carhire-algarve.com* (pick-up point in Vila Real is shown.)
Reserve a zip line at *mobile tel. 0034 670 313 933* or *www.limitezero. com*

Phoenicians, Romans and the Moors all used the Rio Guadiana for transporting gold, silver and copper from the mines around. The loading point at Mértola, with its gleaming white houses stretching up the castle hillside above the river, is the focal point of this one-day tour which also takes you into Alentejo, the Algarve's neighbouring region to the north.

`09:30am` Start this tour with a visit to **❶ Castro Marim** → **p. 72**, 6 km/3.7 miles to the north of Vila Real. From far in the distance, you can spot the main **castelo** perching on a hill. It is well worth a visit and takes you high up to the town. The castle was home to the influential Order of Christ back in the 14th century and today the well-maintained ruins offer a splendid sight over the Rio Guadiana lowlands and the natural reserve Reserva Natural do Sapal de Castro Marim → p. 73 where flamingos have also settled.

`11:00am` After visiting the castle, **head north on the N 122 (IC 27). Approximately 12 km/7.5 miles after Castro Marim, turn right to Foz de Odeleite (signposted)** taking the tidal coast road along the wide **Rio Guadiana** → **p. 73** with splendid views to accompany you! The river is 744 km/462 miles long yet only the last 50 km/30 miles before the mouth of the sea are navigable waters. The neighbouring valleys are home to many species of birds, including more seldom varieties. Take a longer break in **❷ Alcoutim** → **p. 72** – Spain lies right on the opposite river bank. Anyone who likes the idea of flying down a `INSIDER TIP` Zipline from one country to the other should contact **Limitezero** *(daily in the summer 10am–2pm and 4–8pm, otherwise Wed–Sun 10:30am–2pm and 3–7pm)*. The zip line is over 700 m/766 yds long and reaches maximum speeds of 80 km/h / 50 mph. The line starts on the Spanish side – which you can reach by ferry sailing at regular intervals; the journey lasts approximately 3 minutes. Otherwise the secluded **castelo** in Alcoutim is also worth a visit. Lying just above the river bank is the village square where you can eat well at lunchtime in the **O Camané restaurant** *(daily | Budget)*.

`02:00pm` When finished, **take the N 122–1 in a south-westerly direction out of Alcoutim and head north-bound at the crossroads on the N 122 (IC 27).** Your

❶ Castro Marim

37.5 km/23 mi

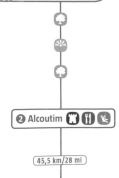

❷ Alcoutim

45,5 km/28 mi

Flip-Flops and a friendly dog: pedestrian zone in Vila Real de Santo António

❸ Mértola

70.5 km/44 mi

❹ Praia de Santo António

route now passes through a virtually uninhabited region into the Alentejo. The castle of ❸ **Mértola** suddenly appears in front of you. Streets wind between small whitewashed houses up to the parish church of **Igreja Matriz**, once a mosque that was converted into a Christian place of worship. The hoof-shaped entrances and Islamic mihrab facing Mecca are the special features of this church. The town's highlight is its castle with impressive tower, the **Torre de Menagem**. Enjoy the view and then a refreshment in one of the cafés in the lower part of town.

04:30pm Now head **south from Mértola on the N 122 (IC 27)** directly to Vila Real de Santo António without stopping. On the last section of this route, you'll notice on your right the reservoir (Barragem) of Odeleite. Before winding down the day here, first drive along this partly bumpy road **for a few kilometres following the river until you reach a right turnoff,** at the end of which is the car park for the ❹ **Praia de Santo António** – a vast stretch of beach unknown to many tourists ex

tending almost to the mouth of the Rio Guadiana and surrounded by sand dunes. After a spot of (sun) bathing, take a stroll around the historical centre of **⑤ Vila Real de Santo António** → p. 71 followed by a break in one of the cafés or restaurants on the wide, lively main square. A traditional haunt is the **Puro Café** *(daily | Praça Marquês do Pombal | tel. 2 81 51 24 99 | Budget)* where you can sit on the terrace, have a coffee and a piece of cake or an ice cold "Sagres" beer and watch the world go by, as the day slowly turns into a balmy summer evening.

4.5 km/2.8 mi

⑤ Vila Real de Santo António

④ THROUGH THE UNSPOILT HINTERLAND

START: ❶ Loulé **END:** ❸ São Brás de Alportel	**7 hours** Walking time (without stops) **1 hour**
Distance: 🚗 30 km/19 mi	**Difficulty:** .ıll **very easy**	

COSTS: 20 euros per person for food and admissions
WHAT TO PACK: Hiking shoes, water to drink, food and snacks

IMPORTANT TIPS: Think about taking sun protection for the hike in summer (headwear)

Discover this sparsely populated inland region by car and by foot. You'll be surprised at the rural areas which the Algarve has to offer away from its bustling coastal resorts: hilly countryside dotted with small towns and cork and holm oak forests. The natural reserve of Fonte da Benémola is rich in water with its sources and streams.

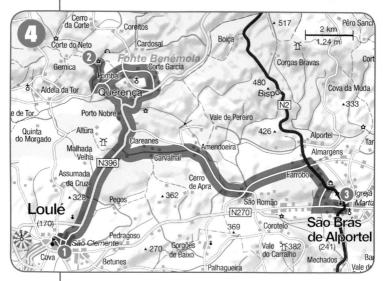

① Loulé 🏛️🛍️☕

(14.5 km/9 mi)

② Fonte da Benémola 🌳

09:30am Start in **① Loulé → p. 74**, by strolling around its Neo-Moorish **indoor market hall** taking in its traditional smells and tastes and stocking up on fruit and water for your hike later – in typical Algarve atmosphere. Wander through the town's streets and visit the **castelo**. **Café Calcinha → p. 76** is a good spot for a second breakfast.

11:30am On a full stomach, **drive in a north-easterly direction to Querença where you then follow the signs** to the small 392-hectare natural reserve of **② Fonte da Benémola**. **In the village of Vale Mulher, stop at the car park directly next to the road.** Here you'll see the sign "Percursopedestre Fonte da Benémola" which marks the start of the circular trail: The 4.5 km/2.8 miles route is signposted with yellow and red markings. On the way, you'll pass the **Ribeira de Menalva**, a clear water stream that flows through the valley and offers a perfect spot for a cooling break.

Now follow the clearly marked path uphill leaving the stream in the valley behind you. You'll hear the rippling sounds of the stream for a while in this valley surrounded by isolated green hills. Enjoy nature, listen to the birds twittering and relax under the shades of the holm, carob and arbutus trees. To your left stretches the valley below and at the end of this trail, follow the small road back to your car.

17.5 km/11 mi

02:30pm Continue on the N 396 and the N2 until you reach the old cork-production town of ❸ **São Brás de Alportel** → p. 62, which is still home to a handful of cork factories today. You'll arrive in the afternoon just when the **Museu do Traje** → p. 62 is open. This is not your typical, dusty local museum specialising in traditional folk dresses! An interesting side wing is dedicated to the INSIDER TIP extraction and production of cork and its courtyard houses a collection of stagecoaches. The museum's bar with its delightful summer terrace is the perfect way to end your excursion.

❸ São Brás de Alportel

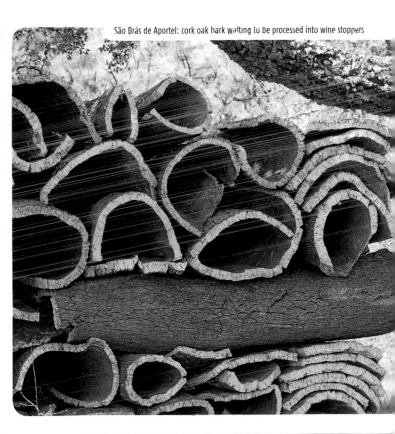

São Brás de Aportel: cork oak bark waiting to be processed into wine stoppers

SPORTS & ACTIVITIES

Stunning beaches and crystal clear water make the Algarve an ideal choice for water sports enthusiasts; it is also world famous for its golf courses.

But there are also a wide variety of other activities on offer – horse riding, sailing, surfing, cycling, scuba diving, snorkelling, hiking, paragliding or stand-up paddling – the Algarve is perfect for them all. Many activities are a little adventurous since often they're all about nature. And if you've booked a hotel with spa facilities, you can enjoy your well-earned relaxation after the trip.

ADVENTURE TOURS

The so-called "safari tours" are very popular: Jump into an open jeep and head into the Algarve hinterland; meet beekeepers, basket weavers and *medronho* distillers. Sometimes, a little river cruise is part of the tour. Some tours have an English-speaking guide. For one day, you experience the simple country life that you wouldn't normally see as a tourist. Most tours take 7 hours and cost 60–70 euros, including lunch.

Do take a jumper – the Serra can be much cooler than the coast. Tours can be booked at stalls in the city centres or travel agencies *(agências de viagem)* or directly e. g. with *Portitours (www.porti tours.pt)*. Another company is *Riosul (Monte Gordo | tel. 2 81 51 02 00 | www.riosultravel.com)*.

From the golfing green onto the surfboard: perfect conditions for golfers and water sport enthusiasts alike

BIRD WATCHING

🐦 The best destinations for birdwatching on your own include the shallow lake INSIDER TIP▶ Lagoa dos Salgados at Armação de Pêra and the Ria de Alvor at Alvor. Close to Castro Marim is the small nature reserve Reserva Natural do Sapal while birdwatchers are also treated to special views at the large nature park of Ria Formosa. Guided tours from *Birdwatching-Algarve (mobile tel. 9 36 12 97 16 | www. birdwatching-algarve.com)*.

CANOE TRIPS

The Algarve's rivers and estuaries are perfect for canoeing. It is much rougher out at sea, when you paddle around to explore the grottoes.

The Ria Formosa nature reserve is where *Lands (tel. 2 89 81 74 66 | www.lands.pt)* undertake their kayak tours. Children from the age of six can participate.

CYCLING

The *Ecovia* cycling route (see p. 52) connects the eastern with the western Algarve – always running as close as possible to the coast. The route, partly very well developed, runs alongside olive groves, salt pans and lagoons. Inevitably, a few sections are close to the busy N 125 road.

and other big sea creatures won't always come towards the boat just as you wish, though – nature cannot be programmed. But still, there's a 90 percent chance to see the animals. If the weather is rough, tours can get cancelled. Lagos marina is a popular starting point where *Seafaris (www.seafaris.net)* and *Bom Dia Boat Trips,* among others, take to the sea. Trips cost

Horse riding is only permitted at specific areas along the beach

Based in Loulé, *Megasport (www.megasport.pt)* offers organised tours and also has several hire stations around the Algarve such as in Cabanas de Tavira. Tours such as from Quinta do Lago–Praia de Faro–Quinta do Lago and Vilamoura–Quarteira–Vilamoura are accompanied by enthusiastic guides..

DOLPHIN WATCHING

INSIDER TIP Dolphin watching in fast, specially equipped zodiacs is available in many places. Common and bottlenose dolphins

25–35 euros per person, depending on the season. Perfect for a family outing!

GOLF

● The British were the first wave of tourists to make the Algarve their dream destination for their favourite sport – golf. They built the first golf courses and in the interim this has grown to as many as 40, each one more impressive than the next. The region is now known as Europe's top golfing destination and international championships held here have elevated the status of the courses. The magnificent rocky coast, while dunes and lush vegetation form exactly the type of backdrop enjoyed by golf lovers. *www.algarve-golf. com | www.algarvegolf.net*

border river is also a very pleasant option. Several companies offer organised charter tours e. g. *Algarve Yacht (www.algar veyacht.com)* and *Algarve Boat Rental (www.algarveboatrental.com)*.

HIKING

The *Via Algarviana* hiking trail takes you through a beautiful 300 km/186 miles stretch from the Rio Guadiana to Cabo de São Vicente. At the Costa Vicentina, parts of the *Rota Vicentina,* coming from the north, are particularly beautiful, **INSIDER TIP** Hiking guide Nicolau da Costa *(Atalaia Walking | mobile tel. 967932206 | www.atalaia-walking.com)* offers guided hikes.

HORSE RIDING

Lusitano horses are a popular choice in the Algarve. Despite being Arab thoroughbreds, they are well behaved and easy to control. Just about every riding school *(centro hípico)* uses Lusitanos. *Quinta da Saudade (mobile tel. 968 05 4013 | www.cavalosquintadasaudade. com)* offers guided horse riding to the beach at Praia Grande near Armação de Pêra, through the dunes and to the Lagoa dos Salgados. The riding stables are located between Albufeira and Armação de Pêra. The horses are very tame. The *Horseshoe Ranch (tel. 282471304)* in Mexilhoeira Grande offers riding holidays for around 630 euros a week, for advanced riders 700 euros.

SAILING

Sailing is a permanent fixture in the south-western corner of continental Europe; there are large marinas in Lagos, Portimão, Albufeira, Olhão and Vilamoura. Wind conditions here are excellent. Sailing down the Rio Guadiana

SCUBA DIVING

The diversity of fish species – particularly in Sagres – is huge and visibility comparatively good. The diving school *Divers Cape (tel. 282624370 | www.diverscape. com)* situated in Sagres harbour offers scuba diving trips.

SURFING

● The fiercer the wind, the greater the delight of the experienced windsurfers – only experienced surfers should brave Atlantic waves. Sagres and the Costa Vicentina have excellent conditions. The best surfing spots are in Praia do Amado while for wind and kite surfers it is the Praia da Bordeira, the Ria de Alvor and Ilha de Faro. Among the surf schools are, at the Praia do Amado, *Future Surfing School (mobile tel. 918755823 and 962557715 | www.future-surf.com)* and *Amado Surf Camp (mobile tel. 927831568 | www.amadosurfcamp.com)* in Sagres and Carrapateira. In Aljezur, you can learn how to surf at *Surf Arrifana (Praia da Arrifana | mobile tel. 917862138 | www.arrifanasurfschool.com)*.

WELLBEING

Many of the higher-end hotels now provide spa facilities with sauna, steam bath and pool. The only thermal baths in the Algarve are geared to tourists and offer all types of accommodation for spa breaks and holidays: *Villa Termal das Caldas de Monchique Spa Resort* (see p. 81).

TRAVEL WITH KIDS

All visitors will be pleased by this: Portugal is a child-friendly nation. Tourists with children will feel this if, for example, a child should cry in an restaurant.

At home the child may draw annoyed looks but in the Algarve someone will probably lean across your table and try to cheer up *a menina* (the little girl) or *o menino* (the little boy).

A great experience for kids is a visit to one of the bustling and colourful markets. The vendors all seem to have a real affinity for children. The most popular markets are those in Loulé and Silves. Even the beaches are child-friendly. The beaches on the south coast are flat and the water shallow and easily accessible. The sand is clean, fine, golden and full of tiny crushed bits of shell and has a great feel to it. Perfect for building sand castles – even the dads can barely be restrained!

Take the children on a boat trip to explore the fascinating and bizarre rock formations between Lagos and Albufeira – an unforgettable holiday adventure. Most of the time the ocean is so placid that the boat will be able take you all the way into the rock caves and your children will be able to peer at the sky through holes in the rock or try to make out the shapes formed by the water reflecting off the rock faces. Snorkelling is another great pastime and a diving course can open up a whole new world for youngsters. Also very pleasant: the many playgrounds and toys, even in the former castle of Alvor.

Perfect family beaches are not the only attraction: amusement parks and zoos are also very attractive

THE BARLAVENTO

PARQUES AQUÁTICOS

Water theme parks with long slides with tunnels, loops and pipes. They are only open in the warmer months, but be warned they can be an expensive outing. Online booking is usually a bit cheaper; very small children can normally get in for free. In the Barlavento, you can choose between Aqualand *(second half of June daily 10am–5pm, July–beginning of Sept daily 10am–6pm | admission 22 euros, children 5–10 years 16 euros | www.aqualand.pt)* on the N 125 in Alcantarilha (137 D5) *(ᶜ H6)* and *Slide & Splash (April–June and Sept daily 10am–5/5:30pm, July/Aug daily 10am–6/6:30pm, Oct Mon-Sat 10am–5pm | admission 25 euros, children 5–10 years 18 euros | www.slidesplash.com)* also located on the N 125 in Lagoa (136 C5) *(ᶜ G6)*.

PARQUE ZOOLÓGICO DE LAGOS (135 D4) (*M D6*)

Predominantly exotic animals, birds and monkeys live in this zoo which was designed from an educational perspective. Their long tails and gigantic eyes make the black and white, red or striped lemurs look amusing. Hornbills are characterised by their long, down-curved bill and brightly coloured feathers. Indigenous goats and sheep are also on show here. The complex is extremely enjoyable and well maintained, highlights include the walks around the monkey and lemur island. You may encounter a proud peacock on one of the paths as well as see pink flamingos on a small lake. The zoo also has a petting zoo. *Sítio do Medronhal | Barão de São João | 8 km/5 miles north-west of Lagos | April–Sept daily 10am–7pm, Oct–March daily 10am–5pm | admission 16 euros, children 4–11 years 12 euros | www.zoo lagos.com*

ZOOMARINE

(137 E5) (*M H6*)

Shows with performing animals are often regarded with scepticism, however this animal and pleasure park is hard to miss due to its size, location and visitor numbers. The park offers all kinds of shows with birds of prey and dolphins while the aqua park zone, Zoomarine Beach, features a sandy beach and water fun along the fast currents of the "rapid river".

Whoever is intent on getting their value for money from the steep admission prices should arrive early and spend the entire day in Zoomarine. Dedicated shuttle service from all the towns along the coast. *Guia on the N 125 | mid-June–beginning of Sept daily 10am–7:30pm, April-mid-June and beginning of Sept -beginning of Oct Mon–Fri 10am–6pm, March/Oct Mon–Fri 10am–5pm (open on some weekends, see website) | admission 29 euros, children under 10 19 euros, children under 1 m/3.28 ft free | www.zooma rine.com*

THE SOTAVENTO

AQUASHOW PARK (138 C4) (*M L7*)

A pleasure park with slides, wave pool, jacuzzi, "lazy river", parrot show and the mini train for small children and toddlers is located north east of Quarteira. *Estrada National 396 | May daily 10am–5pm, June/Sept 10am–5:30pm, July 10am–6:30pm, Aug 10am–7pm | admission 28 euros, children 5–10 years 19 euros | www.aquashowparkhotel.com*

KARTING ALMANCIL (138 C4) (*M L7*)

The circuit is perfect for children and young adults to put their driving skills to the test in vehicles of different categories. *On the N 125 | Almancil | May–Sept daily, Oct Sat/Sun, Nov–April Tue–Sun mostly 10am–6pm, longer in the summer | 10 minutes in a junior cart 11 euros, in more high-power vehicles up to more than 20 euros | www.kartingalgarve.com*

RIA FORMOSA ENVIRONMENTAL EDUCATION TRAIL ● ⊛

A stunning circle loop starts at the *Quinta de Marim* part of the nature reserve near Olhão (140 A5) (*M O7*). The info point in the parking lot offers a map (usually also in English). With this, you can hike on an apprixmately 4 km/2.5 miles long education trail leading through pine forests and marshland, past vast lagoons, a tidal mill that is still running and, lastly, past salt works and ruins along the way. It's not worth going to the park's information centre first. Much more important: Look out for birds. The children will particularly love the storks.

THE HINTERLAND

KRAZY WORLD

(137 E4) (⊞ J6)

Live shows with reptiles and exotic animals, pony riding, minigolf, crag, swiimming pools and restaurants. *North of Algoz | daily 10am–6pm, in the summer until 6:30pm | admission 10.95 euros, children 5–12 years 6.75 euros | www.krazyworld. com*

PARQUE DA MINA

(136 B3) (⊞ F5)

The residential estate at the foot of the Serra de Monchique once belonged to a mine owner and has now been transformed into a museum. Its collections of clocks and musical instruments are particularly interesting. The tour around the large estate takes you to a ⬩⬩ viewpoint *(miradouro)*, a children's play area, bird aviaries and pens stabling ponies, donkeys and pot belly pigs. The entrance building sells bags of food to feed the animals. *On the road Portimão–Caldas de Monchique, signposted branch | April–Sept daily 10am–7pm, Okt–March 10am–5pm; Nov–Jan Tue–Sun 10am–5pm | admission 10 euros, children 4–11 years 6 euros, family ticket 26 euros*

THE WEST COAST

DONKEY HIKING TRAILS ⊙

(132 A6) (⊞ C4)

Children will happily go on a hike when they know they can have a friendly donkey as their travel companion. *Burros & Artes (tel. 2 82 99 50 68 | burros.artes@ gmail.com)* in Aljezur offers short donkey hiking trails (1.5 hours, half a day or a full day) through the Algarve hinterland from Aljezur to the coast. Dates and prices available on request.

Red mane: riding a Lusitano is a special experience

FESTIVALS & EVENTS

FESTIVALS & EVENTS

JANUARY

Festa dos Chouriços in Querença near Loulé: two-day sausage feast (middle of the month) – of course with samples!

FEBRUARY

Carnival with several processions in Loulé, Quarteira, Moncarapacho, Monte Gordo, Lagos, Paderne, Tavira: Plenty of samba dancing, laughing and drinking... In Alte, the whole town is on the move – a very INSIDER TIP authentic carnival

MARCH/APRIL

Feira dos Enchidos Tradicionais da Serra in Monchique: ham, sausages and everything from the pig. All restaurants compete with hearty dishes (March).
Festa da Mãe Soberana in Loulé is the Algarve's biggest religious festival, it begins with a grand procession at Easter

APRIL

Semana Cultural in Alte: Diverse week of culture from April 25 to May 1 with dances, concerts and more besides

MAY

Festa da Espiga (ear festival) in Salir: ears of corn and olive twigs on the doors symbolise bread and oil; there's folklore and *medronho*
Festival Islâmico in Mértola on the Rio Guadiana. *www.festivalislamicodemer tola.com*

JUNE

Santos Populares processions in different towns devoted to the most popular patron saints such as Santo António, São Pedro and São João
Festival Mediterrâneo in Loulé: world music with musicians from the entire Mediterranean area

JULY

Feira do Presunto: Ham festival in Monchique
Verão em Tavira (summer in Tavira): Programme of entertainment on the Praça da República (until August)
Start of the large INSIDER TIP *summer exhibition* in der Galeria Arte Algarve in Lagoa (bis Anfang Sept featuring special events at the Galeria Arte Algarve in Lagoa (until the start of Sept)

Pop concerts, processions, pomp and ceremony: be it religious, pagan or secular – the Algarve is always up for a festival

AUGUST

INSIDER TIP *Dias Medievais (medieval days)* in Castro Marim and *Feira Medieval* in Silves – the Middle Ages are alive!
Festival do Marisco: shellfish lovers head to Olhão on their annual pilgrimage. www.festivaldormarisco.com
Festival da Sardinha in Portimão – everything revolves around the small delectable sardine
Fatacil in Lagoa: the Algarve's biggest regional fair is accompanied by cultural events
Folk Faro is Faro's international folklore festival

SEPTEMBER

Village festival (Feira) in Marmelete (1st Sun)
Festa do Pescador: Folkloric fishermen's festival in Albufeira

OCTOBER

Birdwatching Festival: Bird lovers from all over the world meet up in Sagres to lk shop and view their beloved species!.

NOVEMBER

Festival da batata doçe in Aljezur is dedicated to the sweet potato (end of Nov)

NATIONAL HOLIDAYS

Local holidays honouring the patron saints as well as:

1 Jan	New Year's Day
Feb/March	Shrove Tuesday
March/April	Good Friday
25 April	*Dia de Liberdade* (Anniversary of the 1974 revolution)
1 May	Labour Day
10 June	*Dia de Camões* (Portugal Day)
15 Aug	Assumption
8 Dec	Immaculate Conception
25 Dec	Christmas

LINKS, BLOGS, APPS & MORE

www.visitportugal.com Is the Tourismo de Portugal website which has an interactive map of the Algarve. Select a town or village and you will be given a number of suggestions for activities, cultural events and a history of the area. The site also has a promotional video – Portugal the Beauty of Simplicity

www.algarve-portal.com Places of interest, beaches, restaurants, weather and events – just about anything of interest for your holiday – can be found on this

comprehensive website. It also has some practical information such as a list of English speaking doctors and dentists in the region. This site also has postings of virtual tours of all the major attractions in the Algarve

www.toursandtracksalgarve.com An overview of ecotourism and outdoor activities (e.g. mountain biking, hiking, kayaking, birdwatching...) in the Algarve

www.goodtimeslagos.com Cheerful website with many inviting pictures and a lot of information on Lagos: What to do, where to eat, what to discover... Also has its own app

catavino.net/travel/portugal/algarve Concise expert information about Algarve cuisine, restaurants, food festivals, markets and the like

algarveblog.net All the latest tips on everything in the Algarve – markets, events, restaurants, villages, beaches... Gets updated fairly regularly

www.expatsportugal.com Everything and anything you need to know or ask. Lots of tips about tax, restaurants, services. Also has an online magazine and chat forum

ahouseinthealgarve.com Edith and her husband moved from London to the Algarve for a year. Reading Edith's weekly posts feels like reading a novel and gets you in the Algarve mood

Whether you are still getting ready for your trip or are already at your destination, you will find more valuable information, videos and networks to add to your holiday experience at these links.

www. travelpod.com Posts and tips of the travel blog community, – sometimes helpful, sometimes less so

twitter.com/#!/algarveandaze Lifestyle, leisure and lusophilia (a fan of everything Portuguese) is the tagline – tweets about restaurants, last minute specials and local events

www.rotavicentina.com Award-winning PR video about the Rota Vicentina long-distance hiking trail, in Portuguese and English

www.algarveuncovered.com/gallery/videos.aspx A wide selection of short videos showcasing villages, resorts, events and up-to-date information promoting the Algarve

www.youtube.com/watch?v=sodmOFBQfqE Impressions of the most beautiful beaches in the Algarve

www.youtube.com/watch?v=dcdOOQTmxIU Interesting short documentary linking big-wave surfing to Portugal's seafaring past

Algarve Golden Triangle App for the "Golden Triangle" millionaires' district between Almancil, Quinta do Lago and Vale do Lobo. Useful information on restaurants, bars, pubs, clubs, leisure activities and entertainment.

Portugal Travel Guide Acquaint yourself with the region through its environment and culture with photos. This App will allow you to find out where the photos were taken and then use them as a basis for planning your holiday, as well as the exact route to take.

Visit Algarve The official app of the Algarve tourist authority, with tips for current events

Portugal Surf Guide Information about the best waves in the Algarve, their location and characteristics. It tells you how to get there, where to eat, where to sleep and where to learn how to surf

TRAVEL TIPS

ARRIVAL

🚗 A rather long car trip so you should allow plenty of time for safe travel. A recommended route is Calais, Bordeaux, Salamanca, Seville and then down to Faro. Calais – Faro is 1,732.89 km/1,077 miles. But you'll be crossing half of Europe, which can be fascinating especially if you have time on your hands. The expensive French motorways can be avoided if you have enough time. There are two recommended routes through Spain: via Barcelona, Madrid, Badajoz or via San Sebastián and Salamanca.

🚆 Only enduring travellers should attempt the journey by train which easily takes 40 hours to reach the most southwesterly point in Europe. However interrailers can enjoy the experience (www.interrail.eu).

✈ The quickest and most comfortable option is to fly London – Faro which takes about 2.5 hours. You can also fly to Lisbon. The train ride from Station Oriente (only 3 km/1.8 miles from the airport) to the Algarve is very pleasant (see "Rail"). Ryanair flies to Faro from several UK and Irish cities i.e. Bournemouth, Bristol, Leeds, Liverpool, Glasgow and Dublin. On arrival in Faro several car hire companies are located in the arrivals hall (see "Car Hire"). Bus lines 14 and 16 travel from the airport to Faro city centre or to the train station. Taxis are also available. All airport information can be found at www.ana.pt

BANKS & CREDIT CARDS

Banks are open Mon–Fri from 8:30am to 3pm. There are ATMs just about everywhere. Rental cars, hotels and many restaurants accept credit cards; debit cards are not as widely accepted.

BUSES

Reasonably priced buses link the coastal cities e. g. from Lagos to Sagres, from Portimão to Monchique, from Faro to Vila Real or Loulé. There are also plenty of buses that commute between the Algarve and Lisbon . Travel time from Faro is about 3.25 hours, fare approximately 20 euros. *Bus station in Faro: Av. da República; in Lagos: Rossio São João; in Portimão: Largo Dique. www.eva-bus. com | www.frotazul-algarve.pt | www.re de-expressos.pt.* The bigger cities have city buses that cover all parts of the city.

CAMPING

Camping anywhere other than in a camp site is prohibited. There are some great

RESPONSIBLE TRAVEL

It doesn't take a lot to be environmentally friendly whilst travelling. Don't just think about your carbon footprint whilst flying to and from your holiday destination but also about how you can protect nature and culture abroad. As a tourist it is especially important to respect nature, look out for local products, cycle instead of driving, save water and much more. If you would like to find out more about eco-tourism please visit: www.ecotourism.org

camp sites all over the region and most of them are well equipped. Look at the camping websites *www.campingeurope.com* and *en.camping.info*.

CAR HIRE

If you want to hire a car or motorbike, you have to be 21 years of age and have had your driver's licence for at least two years. As a rule one has to pay by credit card and you will need to pay a deposit. A far cheaper alternative than hiring cars directly in Portugal is to book a vehicle in advance of your holiday from an international hire car agency. Their prices and services are straightforward and you can cancel up to 24 hours before the hire date at no cost. Prices start from 85 euros a week off-season; however prices can rise considerably during the main season especially if you do not book in advance. The car hire companies have offices and parking bays at the airport in Faro. Whoever plans to drive on the A 22 motorway must hire a transponder from the car hire agency (approx. 1.50 euros a day) which is used to add up the toll fees.

CONSULATES AND EMBASSIES

BRITISH CONSULATE IN PORTIMÃO
Largo Francisco A Mauricio 7–1 | 8500-355 Portimao | Faro | tel. 282490750 | www.gov.uk/government/world/organisations/british-embassy-lisbon

UNITED STATES EMBASSY IN LISBON
Av. das Forças Armadas | Sete-Rios | 1600-081 | Lisbon | tel. 217702122 | http://portugal.usembassy.gov/service.html

CUSTOMS

EU citizens can import and export goods for their personal use tax-free (800 cigarettes, 1 kg tobacco, 90 L of wine, 10 L of spirits over 22 %).
Visitors from other countries must observe the following limits, except for items for personal use. Duty free are: max. 50 g perfume, 200 cigarettes, 50 cigars, 250 g tobacco, 1 L of spirits (over 22 % vol.), 2 L of spirits (under 22 % vol.), 2 L of any wine. Gifts to the value of up to 175 euros may be brought into Portugal.

DRIVING

Always have the following with you when on the road: your driver's license, vehicle registration certificate, insurance certificate, reflective vest and advance warning triangle. Seat belts must also be worn by passengers in the back seat and toddlers require safety seats.
You are urged to be extra vigilant as Portugal drives on the right and the multilane roundabouts can pose a special challenge. If you park illegally you risk having your car removed or clamped. Fines for traffic offences are substantial. Especially if you are caught using your mobile/cell phone while driving. The legal alcohol limit is 0.5. The maximum speed limit in built-up areas is 50 km (31 miles)/hour, 90 km (55 miles)/hour in rural and non-built-up areas and 120 km (74 miles)/hour on the motorway. The A 22 motorway is a toll road however you will not encounter any pay stations. The electronic toll system is complicated: rental cars should be fitted with the necessary connections required to install an electronic transponder. Foreign vehicles

must stop at an electronic dispenser station as soon as they cross the border from Spain heading to Guadiana on the A 22. Drivers must then supply their registration plate and credit card details. The number of toll stations they drive through during their holiday will be automatically debited from their credit card. Go to *www.portu galtolls.com* for more information.

DRINKING WATER

Tap water is safe to drink. In the coastal towns however it may taste of chlorine but it tastes far better in the Algarve hinterland. Reasonably priced bottled water can be bought in 1.5 or 5 litre bottles at all supermarkets.

ELECTRICITY

The Algarve has the same 220 volt as most European countries. You will need an adapter if you want to use a UK plug.

EMERGENCY SERVICES

Phone 112 for police, fire brigade and ambulance.

FOREST FIRE HAZARD

The Algarve hinterland is notorious for dangerous forest fires. The Serra de Monchique and Serra do Caldeirão with their large tracts of eucalyptus, cork oaks and pine trees are particularly vulnerable. In the height of summer bushes and brushwood make for excellent tinder and smoking and open fires are prohibited. Forest police in special vehicles are always on standby.

HEALTH

If you are a UK resident, before going abroad apply for Free European Health Insurance Card (EHIC) from the NHS, which will allow you access to medical treatment while travelling in the Algarve. When in Portugal this means that you can approach the ER *(urgências)* of local health care institutions *(Centros de Saúde)* or state-run hospitals *(hospital)* for treatment. There are state-run hospitals in *Faro (Rua Leão Penedo | tel. 2 89 89 11 00), Portimão (Sítio do Poço Seco | tel. 2 82 45 03 00)* and *Lagos (Rua Castelo dos Governadores | tel. 2 82 77 01 00)*, and Faro and Portimão both have a special paediatric unit for emergencies *(urgência pediátrica)*. Long delays can be expected.

Private medical travel insurance is recommended, as it allows you to be treated by a private hospital or a doctors' practice where waiting times will be shorter and where English is also often spoken. You may however have to pay your bill upfront so it is imperative that you keep all treatment and medication invoices. Private hospitals belonging to the *Hospital Particular do Algarve (www.grupohpa. com)* group are found in Faro, Portimão and Alvor. Pharmacies *(farmácias)* are open Mon–Fri 9am–7pm, Sat 9am–1pm, longer in the cities. *NB* take the packaging of any medication you take with you on your trip.

HOSTELS

The *pousadas da juventude* are generally functional, clean and attract youngsters from around the world. The Algarve has hostels in Arrifana (Aljezur), Lagos, Portimão, Faro, Tavira and Alcoutim. Information can be obtained from the umbrella organisation *Movijovem (Lisbon | tel. 2 17 23 21 00 | microsites.juven tude.gov.pt)*.

INFORMATION

PORTUGUESE NATIONAL TOURIST OFFICE

11 Belgrave Square | London, SW1X 8PP | 020 7201 6666 | www.visitportugal.com | www.visitalgarve.pt

The Algarve's cities and bigger towns all have their own centrally located tourist information office *(Posto de Turismo)* even if many of them unfortunately do not have much in the way of material. That said, the helpful "Algarve Guia" is available free of charge which lists all events to be held in the Algarve and is published every month.

www.visitalgarve.pt is the official online tourism site for the Algarve. Despite some of the posts written in an overtly advertising style, you can find a whole host of useful information and brochures to download. The separate municipality websites follow the following website address pattern: *www.cm-[resortname].pt*.

MARKETS

Every city has a regional market or *mercado municipal* where fresh fruit, vegetables, meat and fish can be bought. Here amid their loud, colourful and picturesque hustle and bustle you will come face to face with the Algarve at its authentic best. Generally open Mon–Sat from 8pm–1pm, the best of these are in Loulé and Olhão. Aside from these all the districts *(concelhos)* hold a flea market once a month where farmers sell their chickens, hens, seedlings and plants as well. Dates in the free monthly "Algarve Guia" laid out in the tourist offices.

NEWSPAPERS

Foreign newspapers can usually be purchased a day after they appear in their country of origin.

The English language weekly *The Portugal News (www.theportugalnews.com)* and the bi-monthly, bilingual *Essential Algarve* are published locally.

NUDISM

Officially there are only a few beaches where nudism is permitted: *Adegas* in Odeceixe, *Barril* in Tavira and *Deserta* in Faro. Otherwise only one nudist beach is permitted per district and it has to be at least 1,500 m/1 mile from the closest town. Going topless is often possible.

OPENING HOURS

Many restaurants tend to be closed on either Sunday or Monday in the winter months. In summer most restaurants are open all week. It is often advisable to reserve a table. As a rule shops are open Mon–Fri 10am–1pm and 3–7pm, as well as on a Saturday until 1pm. Big supermar-

BUDGETING

Coffee	from 0.60 euros	*for an espresso*
Snack	from 2.50 euros	*for a bifana roll*
Wine	from 2 euros	*for a glass of wine in a bar (red/white/Vinho verde)*
Souvenir	6 euros	*for a handpainted azulejo tile*
Public transport	approx. 1.50 euros	*for 10 km/6 miles railway journey*
Bicycle	15 euros	*Rental fee for a mountain-bike for 1 day*

kets are open seven days a week, mostly 9am–10pm. Museums and places of interest are often closed on a Monday. Some museums and other institutions change their opening hours up to five times a year.

PHONE & MOBILE PHONE

Nine-digit numbers are used countrywide (also for mobile phones). The former dialling codes have been integrated into the numbers. There are payphones everywhere; post offices sell code cards (with code on the receipt) from 5 euros. *UK dialling code +44 | United States +1 | Ireland +353 | Portugal +351.* Prepaid phone cards can be bought in the shops of the mobile phone companies as well as in kiosks and post offices.

POST

Post offices are called *CTT* or *correios* and are open Mon–Fri 8am–6pm, main post offices also on a Saturday morning. Normal letters and postcards within the EU wil take 4–6 days. Postage: *www.ctt.pt.*

PRICES

Museum entrance fees start at 1.50 euros. Set menus in simple local restaurants may include a glass of wine and cost upwards of 9–10 euros.

RAIL

You can explore almost the entire Algarve coastline by rail. Some cities have centrally located train stations e. g. Faro, Tavira, Portimão and Lagos. The Vila Real–Faro journey takes about 75 minutes, Lagos–Faro takes approximately 105 minutes, prices are cheap: 5.20/7.30 euros. Tunes (137 F 5) *(ꞷ J6)* is the Algarve's most central station and the junction between trains from Faro and Lagos. If you are heading from Lagos, this is where to change trains for Lisbon. From Faro the train goes directly on to Lisbon. The high speed train that does the trip regularly from Faro and Lisbon takes three hours and costs 22.20 euros. For timetables and prices go to *www.cp.p* or enquire at the Postos Turismos or directly at the train station.

CURRENCY CONVERTER

£	€	€	£
1	1.40	1	0.72
3	4.17	3	2.15
5	6.96	5	3.59
13	18.08	13	9.34
40	55.65	40	28.75
75	104	75	53.89
120	167	120	86
250	348	250	180
500	696	500	359

$	€	€	$
1	0.92	1	1.09
3	2.75	3	3.27
5	4.58	5	5.45
13	11.92	13	14.18
40	36.67	40	43.64
75	69	75	81.82
120	110	120	131
250	229	250	273
500	458	500	545

For current exchange rates see www.xe.com

SWIMMING

Beaches fly a variety of different coloured flags. Here is what they mean: green flag – good conditions for swimming; yellow flag – warns of changing tides, swells and changing weather; red flag – swimming prohibited; chequered flag – no lifeguards currently on duty. Many beaches in the Algarve are regularly awarded the Blue Flag – the European seal of approval for excellent water quality and clean beaches, issued yearly.

TAXI

The taxi metre will show the exact fare. Transporting of wheelchairs, walkers and prams may not be declined and is free of charge. Surcharge for suitcases.

TIME

Portugal and the UK are in the same time zone, seven hours ahead of US Eastern Time and seven hours behind Australian Eastern Time.

TIPPING

Excessive tipping is almost an insult. 5–10 percent are appropriate in restaurants, bars and cafés if the service warrants it. The tip is left on the table.

WEATHER & WHAT TO WEAR

Europe's most south-westerly region lies on the Atlantic Ocean, but has a mild Mediterranean climate and does not get snow in the winter. During the summer months between May and October it can get particularly hot. Even so it is wise to pack a jumper or jacket for cool summer evenings. It practically never rains in summer although showers may occur during transition periods between the seasons, so well worth packing a raincoat.

WEATHER IN FARO

	Jan	Feb	March	April	May	June	July	Aug	Sept	Okt	Nov	Dec
Daytime temperatures in °C/°F	15/59	16/61	18/64	20/68	22/72	25/77	28/84	28/84	26/79	22/72	18/66	16/61
Night time temperatures in °C/°F	9/48	10/50	11/52	13/55	14/57	18/64	20/68	20/68	18/66	16/61	13/55	10/50
Sunshine hours/day	6	7	7	9	10	12	12	12	10	8	6	6
Precipitation days/month	7	6	8	5	3	1	0	0	2	4	7	7
Water temperature in °C/°F	15/59	15/59	15/59	16/61	17/63	18/64	19/66	20/68	20/68	19/66	17/63	16/61

USEFUL PHRASES PORTUGUESE

PRONUNCIATION

To help you say the Portuguese words we have added a simple pronunciation guide in square brackets and an apostrophe ' before the syllable that is stressed. Note the following sounds shown in the pronunciation guide:
"zh" like the "s" in "pleasure", "ng" indicates a nasal sound at the end of a word (i.e. not with distinct consonants as in English) , e.g. "não" is shown as "nowng", "ee" as in "fee", "ai" as in "aisle", "oo" as in "zoo"

IN BRIEF

Yes/No/Maybe	sim [seeng]/não [nowng]/talvez [tal'vesh]
Please	se faz favor [se fash fa'vor]
Thank you	obrigado (m)/obrigada (f) [obri'gadoo/obri'gada]
Sorry/ Excuse me, please	Desculpa! [dish'kulpa]/Desculpe! [dish'kulp]
May I...?/ Pardon?	Posso...? ['possoo]/ Como? ['komoo]
I would like to ...	Queria... [ke'ria]
Have you got...?	Tem...? [teng]
How much is...	Quanto custa ...? ['kwantoo 'kooshta]
good/bad/broken/ doesn't work	bem [beng]/mal [mal]/estragado [ishtra'gadoo]/ não funciona [nowng fung'siona]
too much/much/little	demais [de'maish]/muito ['mooitoo]/pouco ['pokoo]
all/nothing	tudo ['toodoo]/nada ['nada]
Help!/Attention!/Caution!	Socorro! [soo'korroo]/Atenção! [atten'sowng]
ambulance	ambulância [amboo'langsia]
police/fire brigade	polícia [pu'lisia]/bombeiros [bom'beyroosh]
prohibition/forbidden	interdição [interdi'sowng]/proibido [prooi'bidoo]
danger/dangerous	perigo [pe'rigoo]/perigoso [peri'gosoo]

GREETINGS, FAREWELL

Good morning!/afternoon!/ evening!/night!	Bom dia! [bong 'dia]/Bom dia! [bong 'dia]/ Boa tarde! ['boa 'tard]/Boa noite! ['boa 'noyt]
Hello!/Goodbye!	Olá! [o'la]/Adeus! [a'dy-oosh]
See you	Cião! [chowng]
My name is ...	Chamo-me ... ['shamoo-me]
What's your name?	Como se chama? ['komoo se 'shama] Como te chamas? ['komoo te 'shamas]
I'm from ...	Sou de ... [so de]

Falas português?

"Do you speak Portuguese?" This guide will help you to say the basic words and phrases in Portuguese.

DATE & TIME

Monday/Tuesday	segunda-feira [se'goonda 'feyra]/terça-feira ['tersa 'feyra]
Wednesday/Thursday	quarta-feira ['kwarta 'feyra]/quinta-feira ['kinta 'feyra]
Friday/Saturday	sexta-feira ['seshta 'feyra]/sábado ['sabadoo]
Sunday	domingo [doo'mingoo]
today/tomorrow/	hoje ['ozhe]/amanhã [amman'ya]/
yesterday	ontem ['onteng]
hour/minute	hora ['ora]/minuto [mi'nootoo]
day/night/week	dia [dia]/noite [noyt]/semana [se'mana]
month/year	mês [meysh]/ano ['anoo]
What time is it?	Que horas são? [ke 'orash sowng]
It's three o'clock	São três horas. [sowng tresh 'orash]
It's half past three	São três e meia. [sowng tresh i 'meya]

TRAVEL

open/closed	aberto [a'bertou]/fechado [fe'shadoo]
entrance	entrada [en'trada]
exit	saída [sa'ida]
departure/arrival	partida [par'tida]/chegada [she'gada]
toilets/restrooms/	sanitários [sanni'tariush]/
ladies/gentlemen	senhoras [sen'yorash]/senhores [sen'joresh]
(no) drinking water	água (não) potável ['agwa (nowng) po'tavel]
Where is...?/Where are...?	Onde é...? ['onde e]/Onde são ..? ['onde sowng]
left/right	à esquerda [a lsh'kerda]/à direita [a dee'reyta]
straight ahead/back	em frente [eng 'frente]/para atrás ['para'trash]
bus	autocarro [auto'karroo]
stop	paragem [pa'razheng]
parking lot	estacionamento [eshtassiona'mentoo]
street map/map	mapa ['mappa]/mapa da cidade ['mappa da see'dad]
train station/	estação ferroviária [eshta'sowng ferrovi'aria]/
harbour/airport	porto ['portoo]/aeroporto [a-eyro'portoo]
schedule/ticket	horário [o'rariyu]/bilhete [bil'yet]
single/return	só ida [so 'ida]/ida e volta ['ida i 'vollta]
train/platform	comboio [kom'boyoo]/linha ['linya]
I would like to rent...	Gostaria de alugar... [goshta'ria de alloo'gar]
a car/a bicycle/	um carro [oong 'karroo]/uma bicicleta [ooma
a boat	bissi'kletta]/um barco [oong 'barkoo]
petrol/gas station/	bomba de gasolina ['bomba de gaso'lina]/
petrol/gas / diesel	petróleo [pe'troleo]/gasóleo [ga'soleo]
breakdown/repair shop	avaria [ava'ria]/garagem [ga'razheng]

FOOD & DRINK

Could you please book a table for tonight for four?	Se faz favor, pode reservar-nos para hoje à noite uma mesa para quatro pessoas. ['se fash fa'vor, 'pode reser'varnoosh 'para 'oshe ah noit ooma 'mesa 'para 'kwatroo pe'ssoash]
The menu, please	A ementa, se faz favor. [a i'menta, se fash fa'vor]
bottle/glass	garrafa [gar'raffa]/copo ['koppoo]
salt/pepper/sugar	sal [sall]/pimenta [pi'menta]/açúcar [a'ssookar]
vinegar/oil	vinagre [vi'nagre]/azeite [a'zeite]
milk/cream/lemon	leite ['leyte]/natas ['natash]/limão [li'mowng]
with/without ice/sparkling	com [kong]/sem [seng] gelo ['zheloo]/gás [gash]
vegetarian/allergy	vegetariano/-a [vezhetari'anoo/-a]/alergia [aller'zhia]
May I have the bill, please?	A conta, se faz favor. [a 'konta, se fash fa'vor]

SHOPPING

Where can I find...?	Quero... ['keroo]/Procuro ... [pro'kooroo]
pharmacy/chemist	farmácia [far'massia]/drogaria [droga'ria]
baker/market	padaria [pada'ria]/mercado [mer'kadoo]
shopping centre	centro comercial ['sentroo kommer'ssial]
100 grammes/1 kilo	cem gramas [seng 'grammash]/um quilo [oong 'kiloo]
expensive/cheap/price	caro ['karoo]/barato [ba'ratoo]/preço ['pressoo]
more/less	mais [maish]/menos ['menoosh]

ACCOMMODATION

I have booked a room	Reservei um quarto. [rezer'vey oong 'kwartoo]
Do you have any ... left?	Ainda tem ...? [a'inda teng]
single room	um quarto individual [oong 'kwartoo individu'al]
double room	um quarto de casal [oong 'kwartoo de ka'sal]
breakfast/	pequeno-almoço [pe'kaynoo al'mossoo]/
half board/	meia pensão ['meya pen'sowng]/
full board (American plan)	pensão completa [pen'sowng kom'pleta]
shower/sit-down bath	ducha [doosha]/banho ['banyoo]
balcony/terrace	varanda [va'randa]/terraço [ter'rassoo]
key/room card	chave ['chav-e]/cartão [kar'towng]
luggage/suitcase	bagagem [ba'gazheng]/mala ['mala]/saco ['sakoo]

BANKS, MONEY & CREDIT CARDS

bank/ATM	banco ['bankoo]/multibanco ['multibankoo]
pin code	código pessoal ['kodigoo pessoo'al]
cash/	em dinheiro [eng din'yeyroo]/
credit card	com cartão de crédito [kong kar'towng de 'kreditoo]
note/coin	nota ['nota]/moeda [mo'ayda]

HEALTH

doctor/dentist/ paediatrician	médico ['medikoo]/dentista [den'tishta]/ pediatra [pedi'atra]
hospital/ emergency clinic	hospital [oshpi'tal]/ urgências [oor'zhensiash]
fever/pain	febre ['feybre]/dores ['doresh]
diarrhoea/nausea	diarreia [diar'reya]/enjoo [eng'zho]
sunburn	queimadura [keyma'doora]
inflamed/injured	inflamado [infla'madoo]/ferido [fe'ridoo]
plaster/bandage	penso ['pengshoo]/ligadura [liga'doora]
tablet	comprimido [kompri'midoo]

POST, TELECOMMUNICATIONS & MEDIA

stamp/letter/postcard	selo ['seloo]/carta ['karta]/postal [posh'tal]
I'm looking for a prepaid card for my mobile	Procuro um cartão SIM para o meu telemóvel. [pro'kooroo oong kar'towng sim 'para oo meyoo tele'movel]
Where can I find internet access?	Onde há acesso à internet? ['onde a a'ssessoo a 'internet]
computer/battery/ rechargeable battery	computador [kompoota'dor]/pilha ['pilya]/ bateria [bate'ria]
internet connection	ligação à internet [liga'sowng a 'internet]

LEISURE, SPORTS & BEACH

beach/sunshade/ lounger	praia ['praya]/guarda-sol [gwarda 'sol]/ espreguiçadeira [eshpregissa'deyra]
low tide/high tide/ current	maré baixa [ma're 'baisha]/maré alta [ma're alta]/ corrente [kor'rente]

NUMBERS

0	zero ['zeroo]	20	vinte [veengt]
1	um, uma ['oong, 'ooma]	21	vinte e um ['veengt e 'oong]
2	dois, duas ['doysh, 'dooash]	30	trinta ['treengta]
3	três [tresh]	40	quarenta [kwa'renta]
4	quatro ['kwatroo]	50	cinquenta [seeng'kwengta]
5	cinco ['seengkoo]	100	cem ['seng]
6	seis ['seysh]	200	duzentos [doo'zentoosh]
7	sete ['set]	1000	mil ['meel]
8	oito ['oytoo]	2000	dois mil ['doysh meel]
9	nove ['nov]	10.000	dez mil ['desh meel]
10	dez ['desh]	½	um meio [oong 'meyoo]
11	onze ['ongs]	¼	um quarto [oong 'kwartoo]

ROAD ATLAS

Photo: Praia do Penedo

Exploring the Algarve

The map on the back cover shows how the area has been sub-divided.
The page numbers refer to the different sections in the guidebook

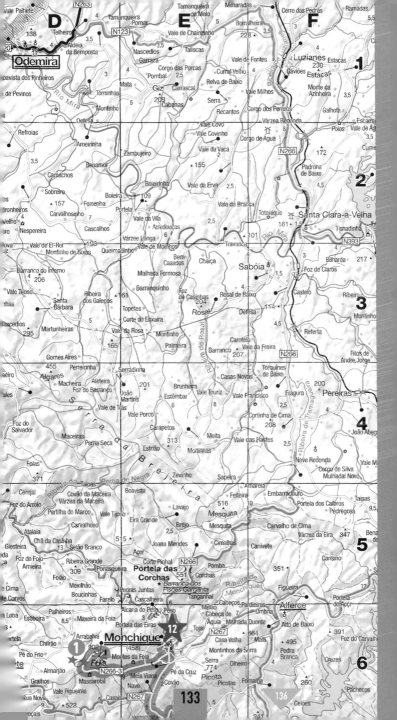

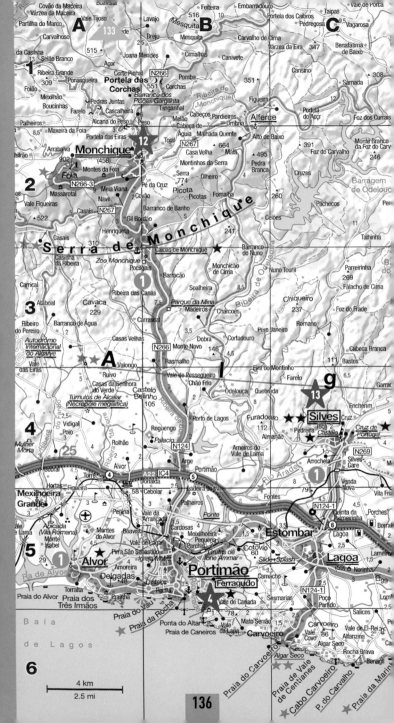

D
E
F
Maxieira
Vale da Rosa
Vales Luís Neto
Barranco
Catraia
Corticadas
Fonte da Pata
Feiteira
Cabaça
Pulo do Cão
Cumeada
Montes Novos
Besteirinhos
Castelão
Vale Maria Dias
Pêro do Livas
Lavajo
Cabeça da Vaca
Cortelha
Carrasqueiro
Parizes
Ameiro
Pedras Ruivas
Javali
Besteiros
Quintã
Barranco Velho
Catraia
N124
Palmeiras
Vale do Covo
Várzea do Velho
Cerro da Corte
Pêro Sancho
Coreitos
Corte do Neto
Cardosal
Boiça
Monte Grande
Fonte Benémola
Corgas Bravas
Corte de Água
Gemica
Corte Garcia
Pombal
Querença
Cortelha
Aldeia da Tor
Bisp
Cova da Muda
Porto Nobre
N2
Vale de Pereiro
Curral da Pedra
Quinta Morgado
Altura
Alportel
Tareja
Clareanes
Malhada Velha
Amendoeira
Almargens
N396
Carvalhal
Garcia
Assumada da Cruz
Cerro de Apra
Mealhas
Bengado
Loulé
Pegos
São Romão
Igreja Matriz
São Brás de Alportel
N270
Corotelo
Pedragoso
Desbarato
São Clemente
Gorgões de Baixo
Vale do Carralho
Betunes
Mechados
Barracha
Peral
Palhagueira
Vale do Galega
Cerro do Manuel Viegas
Santa Catarina
Pinheiro
Goldra
Chameca
Agostos
Fialho
Lagos e Relva
Bemposta
Murta
IP1
Quartos
Canal
Azinheiro
Alfarrobeira
Valados
Vermelhos
Santa Bárbara de Nexe
Guilhim
Cruz da Espragueira
Palácio de Estói
Vale Formoso
E01
A22
Loulé-sul/ Faro aeroporto
Serra de Monte Figo
Vale Grande
São Miguel
Pousada de Faro
São Lourenço
Estádio do Algarve
Falfosa
Ruínas de Milreu
Estói
Almancil
Esteval
Guilhim
Via do Infante de Sagres
Igreja de São Lourenço
N125
São João da Venda
Mata Lobos
Arjona
Rota de Washington Irving
Vale da Venda
Besouro
Alecrineira
Quinta do Lago
Quinta do Ludo
IC4
Conceição
Pechão
Patacão
Mar e Guerra
Vale da Mó
Brancanes
Pinheiros Altos
Biogal
Arrunhado
Ribeira de São Lourenço
N2
Campina
Torre de Natal
Brejo
N2-6
Ludo
Quinta do Gondra
Monte Negro
Rio Seco
Joinal
N125
Marchil
Igreja do Carmo
Olhão
FAO
Aeroporto de Faro
Museu Arqueológico
Praia de Faro
FARO
Catedral
Parque Natural da Ria Formosa
Canal de Faro
Canal de Olhão
Ilha de Faro
Ilha da Culatra
Ilha Deserta
Cabo de Santa Maria
Praia de Farol

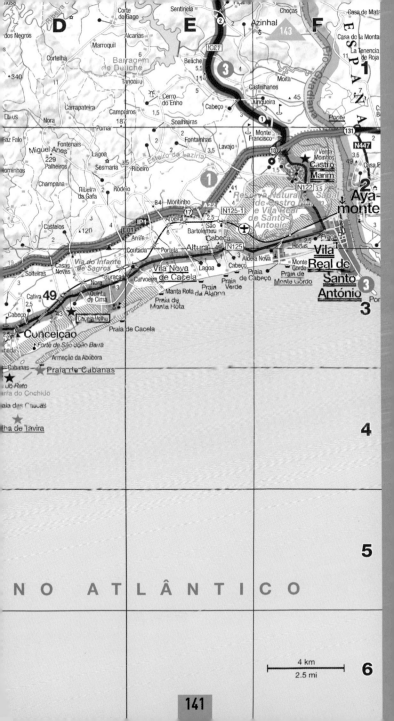

dos Negros

D Corte do Gago
Sentinela
Picarra
Choças
Casa de Mato

Alcarias
Azinhal
143
F
Casa de la Monta

Marroquil

Cortelha
Barragem de Beliche
Beliche 5,5
ICEY
Castelhanos
La Tenencia de Roja

340

Tanoniu
114
Moita

Carrapateira
Campairos
Cerro do Enho
187
Cabeço
Junqueira
45
131
N447

Dius
Nora
Pomar
Soalheiras
1,5

Faz Falo
Fontenais
Miguel Anes
229
Palheiros
Lagoa
Sesmaria
Ribeiro
Fontainhas
Lavajo
Monte Francisco
Castro Marim
N122 3,5

Champana
Ribeira da Gafa
Rôdeio
Esteiro da Laziria
Reserva Natural do Sapal de Castro Marim e Vila Real de Santo António
Aya-monte

Castelos
120
Montinho
84
A22
N125-1
Praça

E01
Aroeira
2,5
São Bartolomeu
Cabeça
Vila Real de Santo António

Coutada
Portela
Altura
N125
Aldeia Nova
Hortas
Vila

Via do Infante de Sagros
Casas Novas
Buracas
Vila Nova de Cacela
Lagoa
Cabeço
Monte Gordo
3

Solteiras
Nora
Curveira
Manta Rota
Praia Verde
Praia de Cabeço
Praia de Monte Gordo

Cativa 49
Quinta de Cima
Praia da Algoa
3

Cabeço
Cacela Velha
Praia de Manta Rota

Conceição
Praia de Cacela

Forte de São João Barra
Armação da Abóbora

Cabanas
Praia de Cabanas

o Rato
arra do Cochido

aia das Chocas

lha de Tavira

4

5

N O   A T L Â N T I C O

6

4 km
2.5 mi

141

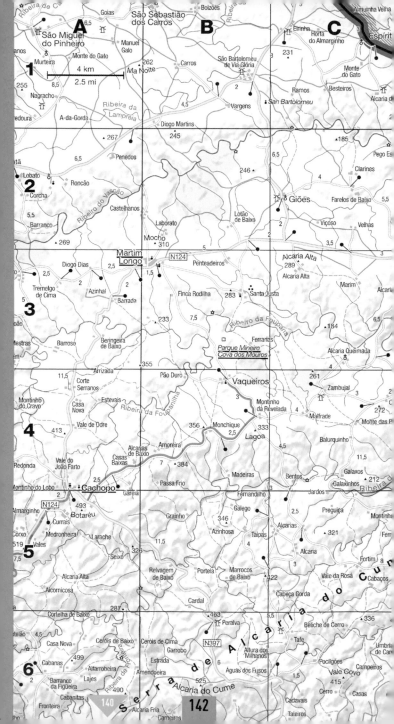

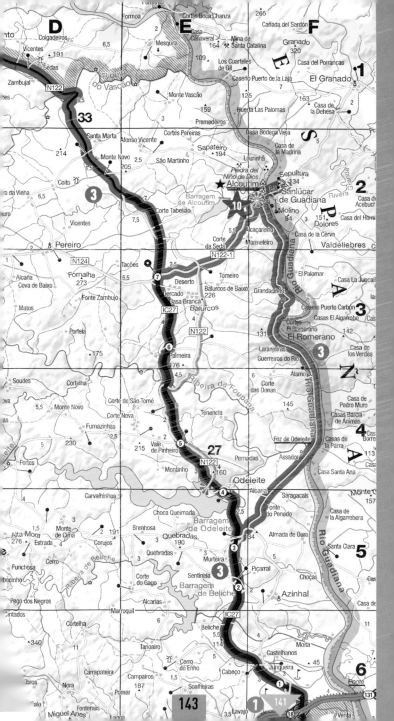

KEY TO ROAD ATLAS

Autobahn · Gebührenpflichtige Anschlussstelle · Gebührenstelle · Anschlussstelle mit Nummer · Rasthaus mit Übernachtung · Raststätte · Kleinraststätte · Tankstelle · Parkplatz mit und ohne WC	Trento	Motorway · Toll junction · Toll station · Junction with number · Motel · Restaurant · Snackbar · Filling-station · Parking place with and without WC
Autobahn in Bau und geplant mit Datum der voraussichtlichen Verkehrsübergabe	Datum Date	Motorway under construction and projected with expected date of opening
Zweibahnige Straße (4-spurig)		Dual carriageway (4 lanes)
Fernverkehrsstraße · Straßennummern	14 E45	Trunk road · Road numbers
Wichtige Hauptstraße		Important main road
Hauptstraße · Tunnel · Brücke	)=(	Main road · Tunnel · Bridge
Nebenstraßen		Minor roads
Fahrweg · Fußweg		Track · Footpath
Wanderweg (Auswahl)	-------------	Tourist footpath (selection)
Eisenbahn mit Fernverkehr		Main line railway
Zahnradbahn, Standseilbahn		Rack-railway, funicular
Kabinenschwebebahn · Sessellift	o—o—o—o o++++++	Aerial cableway · Chair-lift
Autofähre · Personenfähre	●—— ·······◇······	Car ferry · Passenger ferry
Schifffahrtslinie	-----------	Shipping route
Naturschutzgebiet · Sperrgebiet	//////// //////////	Nature reserve · Prohibited area
Nationalpark · Naturpark · Wald		National park · natural park · Forest
Straße für Kfz. gesperrt	X X X X X X	Road closed to motor vehicles
Straße mit Gebühr	·············	Toll road
Straße mit Wintersperre	‖ ‖ ‖ XII-II	Road closed in winter
Straße für Wohnanhänger gesperrt bzw. nicht empfehlenswert	▨ ◁▨ ▨ ◁▨	Road closed or not recommended for caravans
Touristenstraße · Pass	Weinstraße ⌃1510	Tourist route · Pass
Schöner Ausblick · Rundblick · Landschaftlich bes. schöne Strecke	⋎⋏ ☀	Scenic view · Panoramic view · Route with beautiful scenery
Heilbad · Schwimmbad	♨ –	Spa · Swimming pool
Jugendherberge · Campingplatz	△ ⋏ ⅄	Youth hostel · Camping site
Golfplatz · Sprungschanze	⌞ ⟋	Golf-course · Ski jump
Kirche im Ort, freistehend · Kapelle	◒ ⅃	Church · Chapel
Kloster · Klosterruine	⍦ ⌐	Monastery · Monastery ruin
Synagoge · Moschee	✡ ⅄	Synagogue · Mosque
Schloss, Burg · Schloss-, Burgruine	⌁ ⅊	Palace, castle · Ruin
Turm · Funk-, Fernsehturm	Ⅰ ⍾	Tower · Radio-, TV-tower
Leuchtturm · Kraftwerk	⅊̇ ⅃	Lighthouse · Power station
Wasserfall · Schleuse	⤙ ⊥	Waterfall · Lock
Bauwerk · Marktplatz, Areal	▪ ◻	Important building · Market place, area
Ausgrabungs- u. Ruinenstätte · Bergwerk	∴ ⚒	Arch. excavation, ruins · Mine
Dolmen · Menhir · Nuraghen	π Ω	Dolmen · Menhir · Nuraghe
Hünen-, Hügelgrab · Soldatenfriedhof	☆ ⊞	Cairn · Military cemetery
Hotel, Gasthaus, Berghütte · Höhle	⌂ ⌒	Hotel, inn, refuge · Cave

Kultur
Malerisches Ortsbild · Ortshöhe — **WIEN** (171) — **Culture** Picturesque town · Elevation

★★ **MILANO** — Eine Reise wert / Worth a journey

★ TEMPLIN — Lohnt einen Umweg / Worth a detour

Andermatt — Sehenswert / Worth seeing

Landschaft
Eine Reise wert — ★★ **Las Cañadas** — **Landscape** Worth a journey

★ Texel — Lohnt einen Umweg / Worth a detour

Dikti — Sehenswert / Worth seeing

MARCO POLO Erlebnistour 1 — **MARCO POLO Discovery Tour 1**

MARCO POLO Erlebnistouren — **MARCO POLO Discovery Tours**

MARCO POLO Highlight — ★ — **MARCO POLO Highlight**

FOR YOUR NEXT TRIP...

MARCO POLO TRAVEL GUIDES

Algarve
Amsterdam
Andalucia
Athens
Australia
Austria
Bali & Lombok
Bangkok
Barcelona
Berlin
Brazil
Bruges
Brussels
Budapest
Bulgaria
California
Cambodia
Canada East
Canada West / Rockies
& Vancouver
Cape Town &
Garden Route
Cape Verde
Channel Islands
Chicago & The Lakes
China
Cologne
Copenhagen
Corfu
Costa Blanca
& Valencia
Costa Brava
Costa del Sol
& Granada
Crete
Cuba
Cyprus
(North and South)
Dresden

Dubai
Dublin
Dubrovnik &
Dalmatian Coast
Edinburgh
Egypt
Egypt Red Sea Resorts
Finland
Florence
Florida
French Atlantic Coast
French Riviera
(Nice, Cannes &
Monaco)
Fuerteventura
Gran Canaria
Greece
Hamburg
Hong Kong & Macau
Iceland
India
India South
Ireland
Israel
Istanbul
Italy
Jordan
Kos
Krakow
Lake Garda
Lanzarote
Las Vegas
Lisbon
London
Los Angeles
Madeira & Porto Santo
Madrid
Mallorca
Malta & Gozo

Mauritius
Menorca
Milan
Montenegro
Morocco
Munich
Naples & Amalfi Coast
New York
New Zealand
Norway
Oslo
Paris
Phuket
Portugal
Prague
Rhodes
Rome
San Francisco
Sardinia
Scotland
Seychelles
Shanghai
Sicily
Singapore
South Africa
Sri Lanka
Stockholm
Switzerland
Tenerife
Thailand
Turkey
Turkey South Coast
Tuscany
United Arab Emirates
USA Southwest
(Las Vegas, Colorado,
New Mexico, Arizona
& Utah)
Venice
Vienna
Vietnam
Zakynthos & Ithaca,
Kefalonia, Lefkas

The travel guides with
Insider Tips

INDEX

This index lists all places, sights and beaches *(Praias)* featured in this guide. Numbers in bold indicate a main entry.

Albufeira 26, **32**, 39, 68, 97, 111, 112, 117, 122
Alcalar 14, **48**
Alcantarilha **36**, 113
Alcoutim 24, **72**, 103, 123
Alferce 79
Algar Seco 50
Algoz **85**, 115
Aljezur 18, 24, **86**, 91, 101, 111, 115, 117, 123
Almancil 20, **69**, 114
Alte 30, **77**, 116
Alvor 17, 19, 47, **49**, 52, 98, 113, 123
Armação de Pêra **36**, 38, 47, 109
Armona **61**, 62, 63
Arrifana **88**, 122
Autodrom 49
Ayamonte 71
Barão de São João 43, 114
Barragem da Bravura **44**
Barragem de Odelouca 81
Barragem do Arade 85
Barragem do Funcho 85
Barranco do Velho 78
Beliche 52
Benagil 47
Bensafrim 100
Boca do Rio 44
Burgau 43, **44**
Cabanas de Tavira 66
Cabo de Santa Maria 61
Cabo de São Vicente 52, 55, 79, **89**, 99, 102, 111
Cacela Velha 66, 95
Caldas de Monchique **81**, 98
Caldeirão 125
Carrapateira **91**, 101, 111
Carvoeiro 17, 35, 38, 47, **49**, 97
Castro Marim 31, **72**, 103, 117
Costa Vicentina 16, 21, 86, 91, 111, 148
Culatra **60**, 62, 63
Douro 29
Estói 61
Faro 16, 23, 52, **56**, 94, 117, 120, 121, 122, 123, 124, 125
Ferragudo 47, **50**
Fiesa 37
Fóia 79, 81, **82**, 98
Fonte da Benémola **77**, 106
Foz de Odeleite 72, 73
Fuseta 63, **66**, 95
Guia **37**, 114
Ilha de Faro 60, 111
Ilha de Tavira **66**, 95
Ilha Deserta 61

Ilhas de Martinhal 52
Isla Cristina 71
Lagoa **51**, 97, 114, 116
Lagoa dos Salgados 36, 97, 109
Lagos 17, 19, 20, 23, 24, **39**, 47, 52, 98, 100, 109, 111, 112, 114, 121, 123
Loulé 16, 19, 20, 23, 30, **74**, 82, 96, 106, 110, 112, 116, 120, 123
Luz 43, 44
Manta Rota 72
Marmelete 117
Meia Praia 42
Mértola 73, 104, 116
Mexilhoeira da Carregação 48
Mexilhoeira Grande 50
Milreu 61
Moncarapacho 116
Monchique 16, 18, **78**, 86, 98, 116, 122, 125
Monte Clérigo 88
Monte Gordo 71, **73**, 95, 108, 116
Monte Velho 18
Nossa Senhora da Rocha **37**, 97
Nossa Senhora de Guadalupe 55
Odeceixe **89**, 122
Odelouca 47
Odiáxere 44
Olhão **62**, 64, 94, 111, 114, 117, 123
Olhos de Água 34
Paderne 38
Pedralva 91
Penina 78
Pêra 37
Picota 79, 81, **82**
Poço Barreto 84
Ponta da Piedade **40**, 42, 98
Porches 30
Portimão **44**, 52, 85, 98, 111, 117, 121, 122, 123
Porto Mós 19, 42
Praia da Amoreira 101
Praia da Balaia 35
Praia da Baleeira 35
Praia da Bordeira 91, 101, 111
Praia da Falésia 32, 33, 35, 36, **38**, 68, 97, 148
Praia da Figueira 55
Praia da Galé 35, 36, 97
Praia da Ingrina 55
Praia da Manta Rota 64
Praia da Mareta 54
Praia da Marinha 47
Praia da Oura 35
Praia da Paraíso 47

Praia da Rocha 46, **51**, 98
Praia da Rocha Baixinha 68
Praia da Vigia 35
Praia de Beliche 91
Praia de Benagil 47, 50
Praia de Cabanas 66
Praia de Centianes 47
Praia de Faro 60, 110
Praia de Maria Luísa 35
Praia de Odeceixe 89
Praia de Santo António 105
Praia de São Rafael 35
Praia do Alemão 46
Praia do Amado 46, 91, 102, 111
Praia do Ancão 56, 68
Praia do Barril 66
Praia do Beliche 54
Praia do Camilo 42
Praia do Caniço 47
Praia do Carvalho 47
Praia do Carvoeiro 97
Praia do Castelo 35
Praia do Garrão 68, 70
Praia do Martinhal 54
Praia do Penedo 35
Praia do Pintadinho 47
Praia do Tonel 54
Praia do Vau 46
Praia do Zavial 55
Praia Dona Ana 41, 42
Praia dos Careanos 46
Praia dos Pescadores 35
Praia dos Três Castelos 46
Praia dos Três Irmãos 47, 48
Praia Grande 36, 47, 51, 97, 110
Praia Olhos de Água, **39**
Praia Quinta do Lago 68
Praia Vale do Lobo 68
Quarteira **70**, 110, 114, 116
Quatro Águas 65, 66
Querença 116
Quinta de Marim 114
Quinta do Lago 17, 56, 64, 110, 119
Raposeira 55
Reserva Natural do Sapal de Castro Marim **73**, 103, 109
Ria de Alvor 42, **49**, 109
Ria Formosa 20, 22, 29, 52, 56, 60, **64**, 68, 70, 95, 109, 110, **114**
Ribeira de Alcantarilha 36
Ribeira de Odelouca 23, 79
Rio Arade 44, 47, 51, 83, 85
Rio Gilão 63
Rio Guadiana 24, 25, 52, 56, **73**, 103, 111, 116

Rocha da Pena **78**
Sagres 24, 32, **51**, 99, 102, 111, 122
Salema **44**, 102
Salir **78**, 116
Santa Luzia 64, 66
Serra de Monchique 78

Silves 16, 18, 47, **82**, 83, 97, 112, 117
Tavira 17, 18, 19, 52, **63**, 95, 116, 121, 122, 123
Vale da Telha 88
Vale do Lobo 70
Vale Fuzeiros 85

Via Algarviana 16, 81, 111
Vila do Bispo **55**, 91
Vila Real de Santo António **71**, 96, 105, 121
Vilamoura 17, 26, 56, **67**, 110

WRITE TO US

e-mail: info@marcopologuides.co.uk

Did you have a great holiday?
Is there something on your mind?
Whatever it is, let us know!
Whether you want to praise, alert us
to errors or give us a personal tip –
MARCO POLO would be pleased to
hear from you.
We do everything we can to provide the
very latest information for your trip.

Nevertheless, despite all of our authors'
thorough research, errors can creep in.
MARCO POLO does not accept any
liability for this. Please contact us by
e-mail or post.

MARCO POLO Travel Publishing Ltd
Pinewood, Chineham Business Park
Crockford Lane, Chineham
Basingstoke, Hampshire RG24 8AL
United Kingdom

PICTURE CREDITS
Cover photograph: Ferragudo (Huber: Grätenhain)
Photos: DuMont Bildarchiv: Widmann (10, 25, 30, 30/31, 62, 69); © fotolia.com: Artmann/Witte (18 top); R.
Freyer (58, 65); S. Hetet (38); I. Holz (31, 74/75, 76, 116), huber-images: L. Da Ros (5, 12/13, 42/43, 92/93, 130/
131), Gräfenhain (1), M. Howard (14/15, 17, 40, 50/51, 61, 67, 80), S. Lubenow (2/3, 29, 41, 45, 104), J. Wlodarczyk
(37); Laif: Osang (110); Look/Pollex: Roetting (118 bottom); mauritius images: L. Avers (19 bottom), Howard (28
right); mauritius images/Alamy (flap left, flap right, 4 top, 4 bottom, 6, 8, 9, 11, 18 bottom, 22, 26/27, 28 left, 32/
33, 34, 53, 55, 56/57, 70, 83, 84, 86/87, 88/89, 90, 96, 101, 107, 108/109, 112/113, 116/117, 117); mauritius im-
ages/ANP Photo (7); mauritius images/Imagebroker/BAO (48/49); R. Osang (79); Tipi Algarve: Calvin Newport
(18 centre); Vila Valverde: Fernando Guerra/Luis Tavares (19 top); White Star: Gumm (20/21, 46, 115, 118 top);
T. P. Widmann (73, 119)

2nd Edition – fully revised and updated 2016
Worldwide Distribution: Marco Polo Travel Publishing Ltd, Pinewood, Chineham Business Park,
Crockford Lane, Basingstoke, Hampshire RG24 8AL, United Kingdom. Email: sales@marcopolouk.com
© MAIRDUMONT GmbH & Co. KG, Ostfildern
Chief editor: Marion Zorn
Author: Rolf Osang; co-authors: Dr. Andreas Drouve, Jürgen Stromaier; Editor: Arnd M. Schuppius
Programme supervision: Susanne Heimburger, Tamara Hub, Nikolai Michaelis, Kristin Schimpf, Martin
Silbermann
Picture editor: Gabriele Forst; What's hot: wunder media, Munich; Cartography road atlas: © MAIRDUMONT,
Ostfildern; Cartography pull-out map: © MAIRDUMONT, Ostfildern
Design: milchhof: atelier, Berlin; Front cover, pull-out map cover, page 1: factor product munich; Discovery
Tours: Susan Chaaban, Dipl.-Des. (FH)
Translated from German by Birgitt Lederer, Susan Jones; editor of the English edition: Margaret Howie, fullproof.
co.za
Prepress: writehouse, Cologne; InterMedia, Ratingen
Phrase book in cooperation with Ernst Klett Sprachen GmbH, Stuttgart,
Editorial by Pons Wörterbücher

MIX
Paper from
responsible sources
FSC® C124385

DOS & DON'TS 👆

A few things you should bear in mind in the Algarve

DON'T IGNORE THE SIGNS

Erosion has afflicted many cliff sections in the Algarve. In some places, warning signs point out parts of the cliffs that are in danger of falling off, e.g. at the Praia da Falésia or the Costa Vicentina. Please take these signs seriously – up on the cliffs as well as down on the beaches.

DON'T LEAVE YOUR VALUABLES IN THE CAR

You only have yourself to blame if your car is broken into because a camera, handbag or other items of value have been left in full view. Be especially vigilant in parking areas at isolated beaches. Make a habit of not leaving anything in your car and see to it that Portugal's crime rate stay as low as it is now.

DON'T ORDER A "PINT"

It can be embarrassing when tourists walk into a pub in the Algarve and loudly order a "pint". You may prefer to arm yourself with a few key Portuguese phrases so that you can order your drink in Portuguese. The locals will certainly appreciate your efforts. At the very least when entering a restaurant or store you should venture a *"bom dia"* (until noon) or *"boa tarde"* (afternoon) in greeting which will be much appreciated.

DON'T LET THE STARTERS SPOIL YOUR MEAL

It may seem very attentive on the part of restaurants when they load your table with sardine paste, olives, bread and sliced goat's cheese but do bear in mind that these items are not complimentary and everything you taste will be added to your bill.

DO USE YOUR THUMB

The Portuguese will never use their thumbs when counting with their fingers. The thumb does however come into its own in a nice little gesture of appreciation for your meal – simply pinch your ear with your thumb and index finger.

DO WEIGH YOUR FISH

Ordering fish or shellfish by price per kilogram? A good idea is to have it weighed before it is prepared so that you don't have any unpleasant surprises when the bill arrives.

DON'T UNDERESTIMATE NARROW ALLEYWAYS

If you're driving, try to keep out of confusing alleyways; better park your car beforehand, or you might find yourself in such a maze that driving through it will require a lot of exhausting high-precision work...